HACKING

THE UNDERGROUND GUIDE

TO COMPUTER HACKING,

INCLUDING WIRELESS

NETWORKS, BASIC SECURITY,

WINDOWS, KALI LINUX AND

PENETRATION TESTING

This document is geared towards providing exact and reliable information in regards to the topic and issue covered. The publication is sold with the idea that the publisher is not required to render accounting, officially permitted, or otherwise, qualified services. If advice is necessary, legal or professional, a practiced individual in the profession should be ordered.

- From a Declaration of Principles which was accepted and approved equally by a Committee of the American Bar Association and a Committee of Publishers and Associations.

The information provided herein is stated to be truthful and consistent, in that any liability, in terms of inattention or otherwise, by any usage or abuse of any policies, processes, or directions contained within is the solitary and utter responsibility of the recipient reader. Under no circumstances will any legal responsibility or blame be held against the publisher for any reparation, damages, or monetary loss due to the information herein, either directly or indirectly.

Respective authors own all copyrights not held by the publisher. Abraham K. White is referred to as the author for all legal purposes but he may not have necessarily edited/written every single part of this book.

The information herein is offered for informational purposes solely, and is universal as so. The presentation of the information is without contract or any type of guarantee assurance.

Table of Contents

CHAPTER THREE: THE IMPLEMENTATION OF WIRELESS TESTING METHODOLOGY   46

CHAPTER FOUR: TEN BEST TOOLS FOR HACKING WIRELESS NETWORKS   63

AUTHOR'S NOTE

Firstly, I want to thank you for purchasing this book.

I hope you enjoy this book and are able to learn more about hacking.

There is a glossary near the end of the book that you can refer to if any words or technical terms are not clear. Also, there are lots of links and programs mentioned in the Appendices that you can take advantage of.

Finally, after you are done reading this book, will you be kind enough to leave a positive review on Amazon? I would greatly appreciate it!

Disclaimer: the information provided in this book about hacking is for educational and research purposes only. The author will not be held responsible for any misuse of the information provided in this book.

CHAPTER ONE: INTRODUCTION TO HACKING

In many countries today, hacking is considered to be one of the biggest national threats. At one time, hacking was like playing with your friend or engaging in harmless pranks on your computer, but this is no longer the case. It is now considered a crime. Intelligence agencies and some countries' security services view hacking as a form of terrorism while governments have condemned it.

In layman's terms, hacking is the act of breaking into someone else's computer to which you have no access and stealing private information by circumventing the security measures. It is dangerous because it sabotages the entire computer system.

The origin of the word "hacking" can be traced back to the 1960's and 1970's. Some hackers, called Yippe, were anti-war protestors and members of the Youth International Party. They played pranks in the streets, and most of their prank techniques were taught within their group. It is important to note that they were involved in tapping telephone lines as well.

Gradually, what was called a prank grew to another level and became known as hacking. However, this time their tools were state-of-the-art mega core processors and multi-function plasma screens.

Hacking tactics are increasingly being used by terrorist organizations for numerous acts of evil, including obtaining illegal funding, spreading propaganda, launching missiles, threatening the government and gathering intelligence about secret military movements.

In this book, various types of hacking will be broken down and explained. Step by step instructions will be provided so that you can protect yourself from hackers in your office and home, as well as on the internet.

HACKER – AN OVERVIEW

This chapter will provide you with the concepts and fundamentals behind hacking. Who are hackers and what do they do? We will also discuss the various types of hackers and their classifications.

In the most elemental definition, hacking can be described as the act of exploiting the weaknesses and shortfalls in a computer system, as well as the network of such a system. In the exploitation of these weaknesses, illegal acts might include stealing private information, accessing a network's configuration and altering it, sabotaging the structural view of the computer's operating system and much more.

Hacking is practiced in almost all countries. However, it predominates in developed countries. The advancement of information and technology within the last two decades has shown that most hackers are based in developing countries such as in South Asia and Southeast Asia.

The term "hacker" is the source of a lot of controversy today and is confusing to many people. Some regard a "hacker" as someone who has the power to make a computer do anything at will. In another context, a hacker is viewed as a computer security specialist whose primary job is to find the loopholes in a computer system or network and fix them. These loophole finders are sometimes referred to as crackers. All of these ambiguities in the world of hacking have made it hard to identify who a hacker is, a fact that also makes it extremely difficult to detect the activity of a hacker who may be playing around with your system.

A plethora of reasons are behind hacking. Some people are into hacking simply to make money. They can steal your password, break into your private information or even alter your correct information and make it incorrect all for monetary gain. Other hackers are in the game just for a challenge or competition. Furthermore, some hackers are the computer world's equivalent of social miscreants, whose purpose is to gain access to a network or system. After gaining access, these hackers will render the network useless so that the users cannot use it properly.

For example, if a community is protesting against something, it can try to hack into a system as a sign of protest against the authorities. It can choose to do this instead of breaking other laws that it considers to be important.

CLASSIFICATION OF HACKERS

There are different types of hackers who have various intentions. Based on their modus operandi, we can classify hackers into the following:

1. WHITE HAT HACKERS

These are the good guys because they do not have evil intentions. Perhaps they are named "white-hat" hackers because the color white signifies purity and cleanliness. They hack into a system to eliminate its vulnerabilities or as a means of carrying out research for companies or schools that focus on computer security. They are also known as ethical hackers. They perform penetration testing and assess the vulnerabilities of computer systems.

2. BLACK HAT HACKERS

These hackers are the "evil" hackers. Their intentions and their methodology violate every definition of "good." Black hat hackers hack with a malicious intention of breaking every rule in the book. They hack for personal gain, as well as for monetary reasons. They are known to be from illegal communities that perfectly fit the stereotype of computer criminals. Black hat hackers use a network's weak spots to render the system useless. These hackers will also destroy your data and information if they are given the chance to do so. When these hackers get into your system, they will threaten to expose your private information to the public with the goal of getting you to do whatever they want. Needless to say, black hat hackers will not fix vulnerabilities in your computer system or network, but will use them against you

3. GREY HAT HACKERS

The intentions of grey hat hackers cannot be compared to those of the hackers mentioned earlier. These hackers will trawl the internet and look for weaknesses in a computer system or network and hack into it. They may do this to show loopholes in the network to the network administrator and suggest ways of rectifying those loopholes for a given price.

4. BLUE HAT HACKERS

It is said that the color blue represents a member of law enforcement, although this is just a convention. These hackers are freelancers who sell their hacking skills as a service. Computer security firms hire hacking experts to test their networks so that they can be checked for weaknesses, vulnerabilities and loopholes before they are released to the public. Blue hat hackers are "good guys" and are different from grey hat hackers, whose intentions may be unpredictable.

5. ELITE HACKERS

These are hackers who are the experts in the community. In most cases, they can break into something impenetrable and also write complex hacking programs. An example of an elite hacker is Gary McKinnon. As a kid, McKinnon broke into the channels at NASA, installed viruses and deleted files. Elite status is conferred on this type of person primarily by the hacking community or group to which the person belongs.

6. SKIDDIE

These hackers are not complete newbies. The term "Skiddie" stands for "Script Kiddie." They hack into a computer system or network by using tools that were created by other expert hackers. In most cases, they have little knowledge about the program's background and creation. They are only there to use the programs.

7. NEWBIE

According to the encyclopedia, the word "newbie" means "A new user or a participant who is extremely new and inexperienced to carry out an activity." Newbie hackers are beginners in the world of hacking. They have no prior knowledge or experience. They hang around at the periphery of the community with the objective of learning the ropes from their peers.

8. HACKTIVISM

This version of hacking is a process in which a community or an individual uses hacking skills to push information to the public through the hacked system. Hacktivism can be classified into two kinds:

a. *Cyber terrorism:* This is called terrorism because the hacker intends to break into a system with the purpose of totally destroying or damaging that system or network. The hacker will render the computer completely useless.

b. *Right to information:* These people will hack into a system or a network to gather confidential data from both public and private sources, making the information accessible to anyone.

9. INTELLIGENCE AGENCIES

Any country can be hacked. To keep a country safe from hacking, intelligence agencies, along with anti-cyber terrorism agencies, engage in their own form of hacking. They do this to protect their countries from foreign attacks and threats. In the normal sense, we can't conclude that this is hacking because these agencies are acting as blue hat hackers to employ a defense strategy.

10. ORGANIZED CRIME

In many crime movies, the villain has a godfather for whom he or she works. Organized crime hackers work for bosses. They are related to black hat hackers because they commit crimes and break laws to aid in the criminal objectives of the godfather or gang to which they belong.

STEPS PERFORMED BY HACKERS TO HACK A SYSTEM/NETWORK

Before a hacker can hack into a system, he or she must complete certain processes. Some of these are:

1. RECONNAISSANCE

To avoid being hacked, you should keep your private information very secure. The word "reconnaissance" in this context is a means by which the hacker tries to gather all information regarding you (the target) and any weak spots in your system. The hacker uses this step to find as much information as possible about the target.

2. SCANNING AND ENUMERATION

In this phase, the hacker uses the information gathered during the previous phase to test and examine your network. Scanning involves the use of intelligent system port scanning to examine your system's open ports and vulnerable spots. The attacker can use numerous automated tools to check and test your system's vulnerabilities.

3. GAINING ACCESS

If the hacker was able to complete the two phases above, his/her next stage is to gain access to your system. This stage is where all of the hacker's fun will begin. He or she will use the weaknesses discovered during the reconnaissance and scanning of your system to break into your connection. The hacker could exploit your local area network, your internet (both online or offline) or your local access to a PC. In the real sense, the moment a hacker breaks into your system or network, the hacker is considered to be the owner of that system. The security breach refers to the stage in which the hacker can use evil techniques to damage your system.

4. MAINTAINING ACCESS

In the previous phase, we said that once a black hat hacker hacks your system, it is no longer yours. In this phase, after the hacker has breached your security access and hacked your system completely, he or she can gain future access to your computer by creating a backdoor. So even if you get access to that computer system or network again, you still can't be sure you are in total control. The hacker could install some scripts that would allow access to your system even when you think the threat is gone.

5. CLEARING TRACKS

The hacker gained access to your system and at the same time maintained access to that system. What do you think the hacker will do next? The hacker will then clear all of his or her tracks to avoid detection by security personnel or agencies so that he or she can continue using the system. In other cases, the hacker may do this just to prevent legal action against him or her. Today, many security breaches go undetected. There have been cases in which firewalls were cicumvented even when vigilant log checking was in place.

BASIC SECURITY GUIDELINES

By now, you should have some insight into what hacking is all about. Now we will outline the fundamental security guidelines that will protect you, your system and your information from external threats. All of the information we will provide is based on practical methodologies that have been used successfully. These methodologies will help prevent a computer system from being attacked and ravaged by malicious users.

Update Your OS (Operating System)

Operating systems are open to different types of attacks. On a daily basis, new viruses are released; this alone should make you cautious because your operating system might be vulnerable to a new set of threats. This is why the vendors of these operating systems release new updates on a regular basis, so that they can stay ahead of new threats. The best way to protect yourself from new threats is to update your operating system on a weekly or monthly basis. This will help you improve your security and reduce the risk of your system becoming a host to viruses.

Update Your Software

In the previous section, we talked about the importance of an update. Updated software is equipped with more efficiency and convenience, and even has better built-in security features. Thus, it is imperative that you frequently update your applications, browsers and other programs.

Antivirus

Based on our research, we have seen that some operating systems are open to a lot of attacks, especially Microsoft or Windows platforms. One way you can protect your system from viruses is through an antivirus program. An antivirus program can save you in many ways. There are many antivirus programs (free or paid) that you can install on your system to protect against threats. A malicious hacker can plant a virus on your system through the internet, but with a good antivirus scan, you can see the threat and eliminate it. As with any other software or program, your antivirus software needs frequent updates to be 100 percent effective.

Anti-Spyware

This program is also important, as you don't want trojan programs on your system. You can get many anti-spyware programs on the internet; just make sure you go for one that has received good ratings.

Go for Macintosh

The Windows operating system is very popular and therefore many hackers and crackers target it. You may have read articles and blogs saying that Macintosh operating systems are less secure; however, Macintosh is immune to many threats that affect Windows. Thus, we urge you to try the Macintosh platform. However, as we have explained in other chapters, no system in the world is completely hack-proof, so don't let your guard down.

Avoid Shady Sites

When you are browsing Facebook, you may come across unknown people who send you messages with links, some in the form of clickbait. Avoid clicking on such links. Also, you must avoid porn sites, or sites that promise you things that are too good to be true. Some of these sites promise you free music when you click on a link, while others offer free money or a movie. These sites are run by malicious hackers who are looking for ways to harm your computer with their malware links. Take note that on some malicious sites, you don't even have to click on anything to be hacked. A good browser will always inform you of a bad site before it takes you there. Always listen to your browser's warnings and head back to safety if necessary.

Firewall

If you are a computer specialist working in an organization, you might come across cases in which more than one computer system's OS is under one network. In situations like these, you must install software that provides a security firewall. The Windows operating system has an inbuilt firewall that you can activate and use directly. This firewall feature comes in different versions of Windows, including Windows XP, Windows Professional, Windows 10 and the other versions.

Spam

You can be hacked from spamming too. Email providers have taken the initiative to classify emails according to a set of parameters. Some emails will be sent directly into the inbox and some will be sent to the spam folder. To be safe, avoid opening emails that look suspicious. Some of them will have attachments that you should not open. Regardless of the security measures taken by email providers, some spam emails will still pass their filters and come straight into your inbox. Avoid opening such emails and do not download the attachments that come with them.

Back-Up Options

Whether you are running your own business or working for an organization as an ethical hacker, it is crucial that you back up your work. Some files will contain confidential information, such as personal files, financial data and work-related documents you cannot afford to lose. You should register with Google Drive, Onedrive and other cloud drive companies so that you can upload your files as a form of backup. You can also purchase an external hard disk and transfer all of your important files to it. Take all these security measures because a single malicious software can scramble your data regardless of the antivirus you have installed. You can't reverse some actions once they've been taken, so always have a backup.

Password

This is the most important aspect of security. The importance of a strong password can never be overstated. Starting from your e-mail, your documents or even a secure server, a good password is the first and last line of defense against external threats. There are two categories of passwords: weak and strong. A weak password is made by using your mobile phone number, your name, a family member's name or something that can be guessed easily. Avoid using this kind of password, as even an amateur hacker can guess it.

Some people use dates such as their birthday or a special anniversary; however, that is still not safe. When creating a password, take your time and do some basic math because your password must contain both letters and numbers. You can even combine it with special characters. For instance, if your initial password is "jack," you can make it "J@ck007." A password like this will be almost impossible to guess even though it's simple. Furthermore, avoid writing down your passwords. Your password isn't a file that needs backup; it must be personal to you. Make sure you use a simple password that is very strong. However, keep in mind that a strong password still doesn't make you completely safe.

GENERAL SAFETY TIPS

At this point, you should have an in-depth idea of what hacking is all about and some guidelines for ensuring the safety of your computer system or network. Following are general tips to follow to avoid becoming a victim of hackers.

- When you log into your email, you should avoid opening emails from unknown sources. Most importantly, do not download any attachments that come with such emails.

- Do not visit unsafe websites. Always visit websites that are secured, such as sites with **"https"**. Try to only engage in safe browsing.

- Before you install a new program, make sure the program is scanned to ensure it is free of viruses. Then, you want to delete any old installation files because you now have the new installation files. This can save you if a hacker uses those old files as a backdoor.

- Scan your files from time to time. Also make sure that all of the applications on your system are updated frequently to the latest version.

- If you work at home, make sure you are in contact with security professionals or firms that can help you check network loopholes and rectify them as soon as possible.

- Always back up your files. You can use safe cloud drives such as Google Drive or Dropbox. You can also purchase an external drive to keep your important files safe and intact.

- Are you on a social network? Avoid clicking on links sent by people you don't know. Such tempting messages can be invitations to private chat rooms or promises of money if you click on the links. Avoid them and stay safe.

- As technology is improving, so are software developers. Always make sure you are surfing the internet with a good browser. For instance, some browsers have inbuilt virus or danger detection bots, which will alert you if you are trying to access a web page that is not safe. When you want to download a browser, go for one with better inbuilt security features. The following browsers are recommended:

a) Google Chrome

b) Mozilla Firefox

c) Safari

- Use the features that matter to you when you are connected to the internet with your browser. For instance, if you are not using Java or Active X while you are connected, deactivate them in your browser. Having them connected all the time is not safe.

- Research has shown that the most secure operating systems are Linux and Macintosh. If the these two systems meet your needs, it is recommended that you switch to them. They are more secure, as they have had fewer incidences of hacking compared to the popular Windows systems.

- When you sleep, you can still be attacked if your computer system is on and idle or in sleep mode. To prevent this, make sure your computer is completely switched off when you are not using it. It is not possible to hack into a system that is switched off.

CHAPTER TWO: INTRODUCTION TO WIRELESS NETWORK HACKING

Technology is improving on a daily basis. Wireless networks are also called Wireless Local Area Networks (WLANs) or Wi-Fi networks. With the improvement of technology, almost all offices, homes, hotels and coffee shops are installing WLAN as a means of connection. Wi-Fi networks are adaptable and useful because of the comfort they bring to the user, their mobility and the simple fact that they can be less expensive, so almost anyone can afford them. Aside from the fact that this network is less expensive, it is also easier to implement than other wired network connections such as LANs (Local Area Networks). Given the customer's demand, users' solutions and the standard a company seeks to have, Wi-Fi technology is real and genuine. We can say that this technology is here to stay. However, the question is, how safe is this technology?

Wireless networks are based on the IEEE 802.11 (Institute of Electrical and Electronics Engineers) set of standards for WLANs. The IEEE is a group formed in February 1980–the same year and month the names were founded. In the name "IEEE 802.11", the ".11" at the end refers to the WLAN working group, which is a subset of the 802 group. In the industry of groups competing for the best wireless network, the best and hottest players in the game are the Wi-Fi Alliance and the IEEE 802.11 working group.

As the years have passed, the demand for wireless networks has increased tremendously and the WLAN niche has been specified for most specialized applications. Today, the use of wireless technology is rampant as everyone uses WLANs. You are using a WLAN whenever you use a smartphone, be it an Android, iOS, or any other operating software. Moreover, if you are surfing the web on computer that is not linked to a modem by an ethernet cable, you can conclude that you are using a Wireless network.

One key point you need to remember is that "**No Computer Network is Completely Safe.**" The widespread use of this technology has exposed computers to many new dangers. As large as the IEEE group is, the prevalence of wireless networks has made them a bigger target than was ever anticipated. The weakness in the Wired Equivalent Privacy, which is known as WEP in the 802.11 wireless protocol, has not been of help either. Quoting Microsoft, it has been demonstrated that the higher you go in business and the more popular you are, the more attacks you will suffer.

With the flexibility that wireless networks have brought into our lives, including convenience, productivity and cost savings, security is a higher risk. The most common security issues known to a wireless network used to be weak passwords, spyware and missing patches. Although all the mentioned risks are still in existence and are still increasing, WLAN has brought about a new set of vulnerabilities from an entirely different angle, such as the birth of ethical hacking. This hacking is sometimes referred to as white hat hacking and is used to defend against unethical hackers.

Ethical hacking goes deeper than just the name; you can consider it to be an act of penetration testing along with vulnerability testing. In hacking, there are many types of hackers: black hat hackers, gray hat hackers and much more. You can categorically say they are bad guys. Ethical hacking techniques involve planning ahead by using the tools the bad guys might use to defend against their moves before they strike. You can counterattack by using complex testing methodologies and following up on other fixes.

In this chapter, we will look at the vulnerabilities associated with the 802.11 wireless networks and ways you can ethically hack them to make them more secure and protected.

TESTING YOUR WIRELESS SYSTEMS

Since their invention, wireless networks have not been fully secure. Numerous weakness which include encryption flaws, authentication issues and physical security problems have been discovered. There are also many tools that can be used to test your wireless systems. Two wireless security standards have emerged to tackle the attackers: IEEE 802.11i and Wi-Fi Protected Access

Wi-Fi Protected Access (WPA): The Wi-Fi Alliance developed this standard which served as an interim fix for WEP vulnerabilities. It was in use until the IEEE came up with the idea of the 802.11i standard.

IEEE 802.11i: This standard is also referred to as the WPA2 standard. It is officially owned by the IEEE standard. The idea behind it is to incorporate the WPA fixes for WEP with respect to their other forms of encryption and authentication mechanisms. This in turn will promote network security.

Regardless of the vulnerabilities of the 802.11a/b/g protocols, these two standards resolved many security issues. The problem with most security standards is that the solutions don't work because many of the administrators are resilient to change and don't completely implement them. When the network has been configured after implementation, admins avoid reconfiguring their existing wireless settings. They want to avoid designing and implementing complete security mechanisms for fear of complicating their network management. These are legitimate concerns, but they leave most of the wireless networks exposed to danger in the process.

Talking about being fully protected, implementing these standards on a system along with other wireless security strategies still doesn't guarantee that a network will be fully protected. Computer networks cannot be completely safe. For example, let's say you are working for a company whose staff installed unsecured wireless access points on the network and you have no idea about them. Regardless of all the standards you have implemented on your network, past experience still shows that most of these systems are open to threats. Thus, you cannot stop learning. Hacking is like an antivirus version upgrade, as you must keep updating yourself frequently.

UNDERSTANDING THE RISK YOUR SYSTEM IS FACING

Before discussing ethical hacking in depth, we should cover some conceptual definitions which we will use later in the book. Some of them are:

Vulnerability: This is a susceptibility to attack or weakness. A good example is a system network that is not engaging itself with encryption or that has weak passwords on its access points. The access point (AP) is known as the central core for a set of wireless systems. Many of the wireless network weaknesses will be discussed later on.

Threat: This is an indication of potential or imminent danger within an information system. Agent hackers are good examples of threats, as are disgruntled employees. Moreover, malicious software could be spyware, which include viruses that have the ability to wreak havoc on a computer network.

These are the basics but beyond them are a few things that could surface when a threat is able to exploit the weaknesses of a computer network. In this case, the action is known as risk. Sometimes, you might even think that nothing is going on with your wireless network that hackers would be interested in, but there are always plentiful opportunities for danger. Some of the risks connected with weak wireless networks include:

- Stolen passwords

- Having complete access to the files that are being transmitted from the server

- Back-door access points which lead the hackers into the wired network

- Intercepted e-mails

- The rejection of service attacks which can cause downtime along with productivity losses

- Breaking state, federal or international regulations in relation to privacy and business financial reporting

- Spamming

- Zombies (hackers who use your computer network to exploit other networks; this will definitely incriminate your and your system)

The dangers associated with wireless networks aren't that different from those associated with wired networks. In short, wireless networks have a lot of vulnerabilities attached to them.

As bad as it might look, if you don't have the necessary tools, it will be very difficult or even impossible for you to know when you are being hacked, even if you are watching from a mile away. The wireless network can operate anywhere; this can include a curious neighbor who is using a frequency scanner to alternate your connection and listen to your cordless mobile conversations. Without a good tool for protection, anything is possible.

KNOW YOUR ENEMY

The vulnerabilities of a wireless network are not disadvantages in of themselves; the problem lies in the malicious hacker who takes his or her time to abuse these weaknesses. This will obviously make life harder for you. There is a saying: "To track a thief, you have to think like a thief yourself." For you to protect your system, you need to reason the way a hacker would. You and your malicious hacker might have an entirely different perspective regarding the planning of the attack. Still, you will at least understand where the problem is coming from and how they operate as well.

For starters, your hacker is likely to hack your system network if your security requires less work to access it. Hackers will usually target an organization that has only a few wireless access points. There are numerous reasons for this, as mentioned below:

- Systems with fewer wireless access points are more likely to have not changed the default settings, which makes it easier for someone to hack into the system.

- Small organizations will have less time for network administrators to watch their operations.

- Small network systems are less likely to have network checking and controls like WPA or WPA2, or even a WIDS (Wireless Intrusion-Detection System). These are the first things a hacker will check out when trying to hack your network.

However, not only small networks are vulnerable to a hacker's attack. In networks of various sizes, there are plenty of other weaknesses a hacker can play around with, including the following:

- Some network administrators do not have time to monitor the malicious behavior within their network.

- Because a wireless network is an extension of its first generation (a wired network), whenever there is an AP, a wired network is most likely behind it.

- Traffic can also be a weakness. This is because if a network is large, it is going to be easier to crack the WEP (Wired Equivalent Privacy) encryption keys. Traffic is the reason why large networks receive high traffic and an increased volume of packets is sent to the server to be captured. This leads to quicker and faster WEP cracking terms.

- Service-Set-Identifiers (SSIDs) are set to recognizable companies or specific department names. This can offer the hacker or intruder insight into which system network should be attacked first.

WIRELESS NETWORK COMPLEXITIES

Installing a firewall or creating a strong set of passwords and having detailed access control settings is not enough to stay protected. In addition to all of the standards and vulnerabilities mentioned above, you must understand that the largest and most tedious obstacles to securing your wireless network are the complexities found within the network. However, no wireless network can be completely secured. There are some things that are not complex but may still be considered an obstacle. For instance, a plain old AP and a wireless NIC (interface card) might not actually be complex, although you can deduce that a lot more is going on at the backend.

The 802.11 protocols aren't developed to be perfect because they have big issues. These protocols don't simply help you send and receive information with optimal management overhead, like the old Ethernet. Rather, the 802.11 protocols are deeply complex. Most of the wireless networks simply transmit and receive RF (radio frequency) signals which carry a packet of network data. The 802.11 network will actually perform more complex functions, such as:

- Encrypting data to improve data privacy.

- Authenticating clients to be sure only authorized personnel have access to their network.

- Setting timing message packets to be certain about client synchronization and to help avoid data-transmission conflicts.

- Checking the data integrity to make sure that all information remains uncontaminated.

As complex as the 802.11 protocols are, their network design is associated with more complexities such as:

- Staying updated with your wireless devices, which may include laptops, APs and PDAs (Personal Digital Assistants).

- The kind of antennae to implement and where to locate them.

- Knowing the exact type of devices that are allowed on your network and also those that are not.

- Adjusting signal-power settings which will prevent your radio frequency signal from leaking outside your residence.

All of these wireless network complexities add up to a multitude of security weaknesses that are not available in the old traditional wired networks.

HAVING THE RIGHT TOOLS

Every specific task in life requires the right tool. You can't browse the internet without a browser. Even having a browser doesn't guarantee that you can surf the web. This is because some webpages are written in a different language and if your browser is not developed to handle such a language, it will have a hard time loading the webpages. You must have the proper testing tools, which happen to be the most important component of the process of ethical hacking. Preparation involves working towards the right results; otherwise, you are most likely to turn your wheels and you won't achieve a good outcome.

The fact that your wireless tools were developed to accomplish a specific goal doesn't guarantee that they will perform that test successfully. Sometimes you will even need to change your settings to achieve the result you seek, or sometimes you might need to combine the result of one with another. There is also the potential of getting a false positive (i.e., your tool says you have a vulnerability when, in fact, there are none) or a false negative (i.e., your tool says you have no vulnerability when, in fact, there is one).

As technology is evolving on a daily basis, below are some of the best tools you can use to test wireless network security:

- Laptop computer
- Google
- GPS satellite receiver
- Network stumbler software
- QualysGuard vulnerability software
- AiroPeel network-analysis software

- WEPcrack cracking software (for cracking encryption)

Many of them are available on the internet. You obviously can't do without good security testing software or tools, but it is crucial that you know none of these tools is the ultimate saviour in terms of finding and putting an end to your wireless network's vulnerabilities. A mix of all of these tools will create the perfect combination for finding the vulnerabilities in your system. More importantly, you need to know how to use these tools and what specific tasks each is capable of handling.

THE FUNDAMENTAL ANALYSIS OF PROTECTION

Before you can protect, you need to inspect. When you get all of these testing tools prepared, that's the time you need to get ready to test them on your wireless network by performing numerous ethical hacks and attacks on your own network system. By doing this, you are revealing to yourself the areas which are vulnerable on your own network. The results you obtain in the process of attacking your network will give you more insight into where your wireless network is vulnerable, and the depth of the security loopholes that are likely or unlikely to be fixed. Below are the countermeasures you can take to tackle the vulnerabilities you'll encounter in the course of your self-system attack.

- **Non-Technical Attack:** These are attacks used to exploit the weaknesses of a human being – lack of awareness, being too trusting of strangers or being too careless.

- **Network Attacks:** These types of attacks can include the installation of rogue wireless APs and dirty tricks that convince network clients to connect with such clients, notwithstanding network server protocols like SNMP.

- **Software Attacks:** Security worries about 802.11 protocols don't end because we should also be concerned about the applications installed on wireless systems and the operating system. They are also vulnerable to being attacked. Software attacks can involve:

    a. Cracking the WEP keys of your wireless network encryption.

    b. Gaining access to your wireless network by playing around with your weak authentication systems.

    c. Attacking by breaking into your wireless network by using default passwords (if your default settings aren't changed) and also SSIDs which can be easily obtained.

THE 10 COMMANDMENTS OF ETHICAL HACKING

Every process has its own rules and commandments. The bible has rules for its believers to follow. Below are the principles guiding the ethical hacking procedure.

1. THOU SHALT SET THY GOALS.

Let's do some analysis. When Jack was a little boy, he liked playing a game called Capture the Flag. He started this game at camp; his camp counselors became interested in this game and they joined him. Later, this game was improved. The counselors split the campers into two teams: one with a green flag and another with a red flag. Every game had a rule which the players had to follow: If you were on the green flag team, you and your entire team would have to find the red flag, which was hidden by the red flag team, and vice versa.

As simple as this game rule was, things could get a bit messy. This was about a single-minded mindset: Capture the flag. This single-mindedness is related to penetration testing, which means the security test with its defined goal or aim can end only when the goal is achieved or when time runs out. Trying to have access to another access point is similar to trying to find the flag hidden by the opposing team. Your opponent knows you will do anything to access the access point, so he or she will do all it takes to protect it because the opponent knows you will circumvent the defences–you will try to "capture the flag."

Is ethical hacking related to penetration testing? Ethical hacking on its own is a penetration test which can be used as a marketing ploy but with more systems, which means there is more than one goal to achieve.

If you are on the green flag team and you want to locate the red flag hidden by the other team, you need to reason like a flag keeper yourself. You would say, "Where would I hide the flag if I were on the other team?" You have a goal to achieve and this is why your evaluation of wireless network security should seek to answer three logical questions:

- What will the intruder do with the stolen information?

- What private information will the intruder be able to see on the target's network or access points?

- Will users on the target's base notice the intruders' attempt?

Your own goal can be very simple in the sense that you might choose to find an illegal wireless access point's AP. You can also decide to locate or obtain information from a wired network in your system. Whatever you choose to do, the point is, you have to articulate your aims and inform your sponsors about it.

"Two heads are better than one." Whatever you do, you will require a good plan to be successful at it. At this point, you must involve others in your plan and goal-setting process. If you don't, everything about your planning process might be difficult. Goals determine a good plan. Quoting the Cheshire Cat's reply to Alice concerning goals: "If you don't know wherever you are heading, any path can get you there." Include investors in the process of setting a goal, as they will build trust that will pay later on in spades.

2. THOU SHALT HAVE A PLAN.

In life, not everything goes as planned. For instance, we don't all have unlimited budgets; there is something that always binds our plans with constraints. These limitations can be time, money or personnel. The idea here is that you need to plan for your tests.

A good plan will lead to a good result. Thus, the following are essential:

- Know what you want to test and identify the networks.

- Evaluate the testing period.

- Evaluate the testing methodology.

- Implement a good plan and share it with stakeholders.

- Wait to obtain your plan's approval.

Don't worry about the fact that people will believe you want to hack a wireless network; share and publicize your plan. If the organization you work for is like most other organizations, it is very unlikely it can oppose the organizational inertia to do anything to obstruct your efforts. Most importantly, do not forget that you are not evaluating your "testing process" under ordinary conditions.

3. THOU SHALT GET PERMISSION.

Don't forget you are performing an ethical hacking. If you do not obtain proper permissions, there is a chance that you will land yourself in prison. Recall the case of an internal auditor who was caught red-handed cashing a payroll check that he didn't earn. When he was questioned, he replied: "I wasn't stealing, I was only checking out the controls of the system." He could have obtained permission to check the system's vulnerabilities before suggesting a solution to the organization, but he didn't, and that act landed him in prison. In ethical hacking, do not go by the old saying that says, "Seeking forgiveness is easier than asking for permission." If you do not ask for permission, you will surely land in prison.

Remember that this permission can be the only thing standing between you and the black-and-white striped uniform. Seek and obtain a get-out-of-jail-free card. This card will serve as evidence that your test on the network is authorized and that you are performing your operation according to plan. The ticket will say that your organization will stand behind you if you are charged with a criminal offense or sued for your actions. As long as you stick to the plan you created with your organization, your card will provide you with organizational and legal support if something goes wrong.

4. THOU SHALT OPERATE ETHICALLY.

Ethical hacking is the same thing as white hat hacking because the intentions and conscience of the hacker are always good. This commandment is telling you that you have to work according to the plan you provided and that was approved. Avoid taking actions that were not authorized or that are outside your plan. Being an ethical hacker defines the goodness in you, so work ethically.

In the process of your operation, every bit of information you uncover must be confidential and not disclosed to a third party.

As an ethical hacker, you must also strive to make sure everything you do in your operation promotes the progress of your organization and advances its goals. If there is something you must change, inform your agency. You might need to change your plans if you encounter something outside your expectations, such as something that poses a significant risk to the organization's entire network. Don't make decisions alone. Avoid performing ethical hacking if your organization's policy or the law forbids it.

5. THOU SHALT SAVE RECORDS.

To survive and be successful in the profession of ethical hacking, you need to have a lot of patience, be hardworking and have a spirit of thoroughness. This is because being an ethical hacker requires a lot of time; in some cases you will spend hours with a computer's keyboard alone in the dark until you become stressed out and tired. To achieve your goals, you might even need to perform some off-hour work. However, this doesn't mean you will have to put on hacker gear or start drinking Red Bull. The objective of all this is to make sure you achieve your goal and become an unstoppable ethical hacker.

The previous commandment stated how important it is for an ethical hacker to remain within his/her mode of operations. You must operate as a professional, which means that you must keep records. You can keep your records via paper or electronically by using the following strategies:

- Log all operations performed.

- Make duplicates of your logs.

- Record all data in your log.

- Record and keep all factual records; even when you think your work is not successful, you should still record it.

- Document and date every test.

In every organization, there is always a need to report your work. Your report can be your outcome, test design and analysis. Be very diligent in your documentation of records and your work as a whole.

6. THOU SHALT RESPECT PEOPLE'S PRIVACY.

You need to treat every bit of data and information you collect with respect and confidentiality. You must guard the secrecy of private information. In the testing period, you will gather information about, for instance, encryption keys and plain text passwords. All this information must be kept confidential and private. Do not, for instance, snoop into private corporate accounts or individuals' private lives. Take care of the information you have; treat it as if it is yours. A good name is better than riches.

7. THOU SHALT NOT DO HARM.

Whatever you do today always comes back to you; this is known as karma. As an ethical hacker, your prime objective is "do no harm." Resist the urge to go too far. Instead, stick to your original plans. Remember that it is very easy to be caught in ethical hacking. If you try something and it works, you will get used to it. However, nothing lasts forever, and you can easily cause an outage or tamper with someone's information or personal rights. Don't go outside your plan's outline.

We will discuss the tools which you can use to perform hacking later in this book, but be sure you read every detail about each tool's purpose and function. Do not jump into using any tool without understanding the nature of it. You should understand that you are setting up a sum of money and the whole attack can create a rejection of service. Before you engage a hacking tool, relax and take a breath; then be ready to read the full documentation about the tool. Of course, it can be boring, but it's one of the prices to pay to be great.

8. THOU SHALT USE THE SCIENTIFIC PROCESS.

This commandment does not necessarily mean you will follow all of the steps of the scientific process. You just have to adopt some of the fundamental principles of the process in your operation. If you adopt a quasi-scientific method or process in your work, you will have a structure and also prevent chaos (activities which can result from a random walk through your network).

The scientific process contains three steps, which are:

1. Develop and select your plan and goals.

2. Make your network capable of addressing your goals.

3. Persuade your organization to acknowledge your work.

The first two steps have been addressed in the previous commandments. Let's take a look at the third step. If you employ an empirical method, your work outcome should garner greater acceptance. An empirical process has the following properties:

- **Set quantifiable objectives:** In the capture-the-flag game, each team doesn't stop until the opponent's flag has been found. The purpose of setting a quantifiable objective is that you will know when the goal has been reached. This happens in one of two ways: You find the flag, or you don't. Relating this to ethical hacking, you have to select a goal you know you can achieve; then associate the selected goal with up to 10 access points (APs) and the broken encryption keys, as well as files on an internal server. Time-quantifiable objectives can include self-testing your system or network to understand how it can withstand up to three days of consecutive attacks.

- **Tests are steady and repeatable:** Consistency is when you self-test your system or network and achieve the same result using different approaches. If your results are not the same throughout, it is not steady. Scientifically, you should be able to file an explanation report for any form of inconsistency or invalid test result. You can also ask yourself a simple question that you should be expecting from your organization: If your test is repeated, would it have the same result? If you made sure your tests were repeated and you kept getting the same result, you can be confident that no matter how many times the same test is replicated, the result will be the same.

- **Test results should maintain consistency:** Your accurate result from a test should maintain a good timeframe (be a permanent result). If your tests are true, they will be received by your organization with more ease in cases in which the tests address permanent problems. If a test can address only transitory or temporary difficulties, it will be of little use.

9. THOU SHALT NOT STEAL THY NEIGHBOUR'S TOOLS.

Always be satisfied with what you have. More tools for wireless hacking will keep storming the software market and no matter how many you have today, you will keep discovering new ones. More tools will be coming out from time to time because technology is here to stay. In the early days of wireless hacking, there were a limited choice of tools compared to the plethora we have today. Take, for instance, Network Stumbler, which used to be known as NetStumbler on the Windows operating systems. It has the same function as the Kismet software on Linux operating systems. There were limited software choices in earlier days. Now, you have more choices, like WarLinux, Aerosol, AirScanner, APsniff, dstumbler, Gwireless, BSD-Airtools, iStumbler, MacStumbler, KisMAC, Mognet, MiniStumbler, THC-RUT, PocketWarrior, THC-Scan, PocketWiNc, THC-WarDrive, WarLinux, Radiate, WiStumbler, Wellenreiter, Wlandump and much more. These are just the free ones available on the internet. The premium tools which you can purchase are AiroPeek, Air Sniffer, AirMagnet, AP Scanner, Sniff-em, NetChaser and Sniffer Wireless. The idea here is simple: If you have more money and time, you can go to the Internet and download the free tools or purchase the ones you need. Do not steal or be tempted by your neighbor's tools. Get your own and become accustomed to them.

10.   THOU SHALT ACCOUNT ALL FINDINGS.

When someone's privacy is on the line with an action or test, they get nervous about whatever might be going on. For this reason, make sure you are providing timely updates on your progress. Avoid keeping people in suspense when they already know you are breaking into their network. Frequent updates are critical. During your findings, every vulnerability you discover must be reported immediately. Such vulnerabilities include:

- Breaches

- Weaknesses that are exploited with anonymous access.

- Vulnerabilities which will have a high exploitation rate.

- Vulnerabilities which are hazardous to lives.

If you detect a vulnerability and you planned to report it but didn't, in case someone else exploits this weakness, you will not be okay because you have not done the right thing.

If you have humility, you will definitely be awarded for your goodness and honesty. Once you detect a vulnerability in your organization's system or network and report it immediately, you will be recognized for the authenticity of your work. This will also positively affect others' assessment of the way you complete your tasks. Your peers can examine your analysis, methodologies, findings and conclusions. They can offer honest criticism and suggestions which can improve your work.

If you find your reports unjustly criticized, just follow these 10 Commandments, as they will help you prepare your reports better.

Furthermore, if you perform a test and are able to detect 30 problems, make sure you report on all of these 30 problems you detected. You don't need to include all 30 problems in your summary, but include them in the narrative. If you are thinking you have too much to report and choose to withhold some of the information, another person within the organization who detects it later will tag you as an incompetent or lazy. Therefore, it is best to avoid this kind of a situation and report everything.

CHAPTER THREE: THE IMPLEMENTATION OF WIRELESS TESTING METHODOLOGY

Before you can say you want to start testing your wireless vulnerabilities, you need to implement a methodology for it. Ethical hacking of a wireless network is not just about scanning willy-nilly for open ports. For you to have successful testing, you need to follow some formal procedures, which should be incorporated into your methodology. These include:

- Gathering IP addresses and domain names as your public information.

- Mapping your network to have a general idea of the structure.

- Scanning your system or network to get a general overview of which devices are active and transmitting information.

- Determining the services that are running.

- Finding and locating specific vulnerabilities.

- Hacking into the system and finishing the job.

We'll discuss more details about these methodologies in the next section. In chapter two, we covered specific goals and how to achieve them, as well as knowing where you are headed to stay focused on completing your test. Don't forget about this part, as it will make your job a lot easier.

Keep a log of everything you are doing. Backup is important. Your logs can also be saved as a screen capture or screenshot, and you can use the Snaglt tool for this (available at **http://techsmith.com**). Sometimes you might not be able to reproduce the same visual samples of your progress; that is when screen captures come in handy. Logging is very important because sometimes you will need particular data on what you previously did; thus, saving logs will make it easy for you to get that data. For instance, your client might notice a security intrusion in what you did for him or her and may want to track the movement of the intruder. With your loggings, you have the ability to show the client the exact moment you performed your operation, including the date and time.

In the previous chapter, we discussed the important commandments for hacking ethically. Don't forget to employ the scientific method in your hacking methodology as well. When you are performing any kind of security testing that involves private information, make sure you are working methodically. Moreover, make sure you are using the right tool for the right task; don't mix up tools. Using the right tool will help you achieve the greatest number of accurate vulnerability results and show you the weaknesses. Another advantage of working methodically is that you will be able to minimize the sloppiness of the system and avoid crashing the system or network. A different tool should be used for a different system, since it will likely have different specifications.

Your enemy is not your friend and in this sense, your enemy may be a black hat hacker trying to bring down the system you are in charge of. To avoid defeat, be flexible in your methodologies. Adapt the rules and regulations of warfare when it comes to your enemy.

In a movie titled *Transformers*, the enemies were called Decepticons and the humanitarian agencies were the good guys. One of the good guys fighting the enemy taught that when they battled against the bad guys, they had to use the right weapon. He was frustrated when things got bad and said, "Why do the bad guys always get the good stuff?" Relating this movie analysis to your enemy (the bad hacker), you should always expect your enemy to use the best and latest tools. Therefore, you should also get those tools yourself. If they are breaking into your network from across the street, you must be able to perform your tests from across the street as well. If they are breaking into your network configuration from across the internet, you should perform an internet test on your network as well. Know that two ethical hackers cannot be alike. If the need arises for you to adjust your procedures and methods, then do not hesitate to do what is necessary.

DETERMINING WHAT OTHERS KNOW

Basically, what other hackers do at first is prod and poke their target's system to find all of the vulnerabilities. You have to do this as well if you want to last in your game. Run different tests from different angles and try to look into your network from an outsider's perspective. Doing this will help you get more accurate results in terms of what your network looks like to your enemy and not just how it looks to you on your system. This is very important in the realm of wireless networks because we don't have the added veil of physical security as we do with hard-wired systems.

Things You Need to Look For

Before you get started with your wireless testing, here are a few things that are very important to look for:

- Software versions

- IP addressing schemes

- Radio signal strength

- Hardware makes and versions

- Specific SSIDs which are being broadcasted

- Encryption, such as VPN or WEP traffic

METHODOLOGY 1: CONSOLIDATING THE PUBLIC EYE

We said earlier that we would further discuss the methodologies we mentioned above. One crucial point or methodology you should know about is that the very first step in ethical hacking is performing a high-level network reconnaissance called footprinting. For instance, if you are asked to perform broader information security testing on a system or network, you might need to look for things like trademarks names, employee names, company files or parent names. All this information can be found or accessed using available public tools such as Google. You can also gather information using your organization's website or by using the trademark office website (**www.uspto.gov**). Moreover, information available publicly might not be as prevalent as it could be in another form of a network system. This is because the wireless network is more localized and infrastructure-based. Still, it is worth your time to see what you can gather out there.

Gathering Information with Google

Google is one of the best tools of the 21st century. Without it, many businesses wouldn't survive. While there are multiple search engines, Google is the best of them all. Google is considered an excellent tool for performing security tests in general. Google makes it possible for you to perform several web and other queries to find information regarding your wireless systems. With Google's advanced keyword search feature, you can perform a keyword search for more detailed query and search results and network configurations. With this tool, you can also have access to forums where you will find people talking about the keyword you searched; you might find someone who talked about how he was able to improve the same network you have. You might also come across reasons why the network was broken. This information will help you make your system or network better regarding security. Some network configurations can accidentally be made public, which will keep a hacker one step ahead in attacking or hacking such a wireless system. Following are some of the keywords you can search on Google using an advanced search:

- Spreadsheets

- Word-processing documents

- Network diagrams

- Wireless configuration

- Network-analysis packet files

- Presentations

- Network stumbler mapping files

The Foundstone company provides professional services in computer security and has neat query tools that can perform highly advanced queries like Google, including queries you might not even think about. Below is the link:

https://ww.foundstone.com/resources/freetools.htm

Searching Wi-Fi Databases

The Internet is very extensive, and different information is available from different sources. However, not everything you find on the internet is true and accurate. Another way for you to find accurate information about the internet about your wireless system is by using Wi-Fi databases. The information you find on these databases can include MAC addresses, SSIDs and more in-depth information that you haven't even thought of but which has been discovered by some curious outsiders or anonymous users. You can start by using the WiGLE database to find some ideas:

https://www.wigle.net/gps/gps/GPSDB/query

NOTE: You will have to register on the website before you can have access to its public database. You can also check if your AP is listed on the site. Once you join the site, you will have the ability to submit various search options or queries, such as:

- Latitude

- Longitude

- Last update

- BSSID or MAC

- SSID or network

Another alternative to WiGLE is WiFimaps. You can check its website at **www.wifimaps.com** to see if your AP is listed there as well.

To see more about your public information, you can use **www.whois.org** to look up your domain name public data. To look up your IP address, you can use **http://ws.arin.net/cgi-bin/whois.pl** (known as American registry for internet numbers). These databases will provide with sensitive information about your wireless system or network–even information you ought not to be advertising. Access those websites and check your wireless details.

METHODOLOGY 2: MAPPING YOUR NETWORK

This methodology will teach you how to create your network map, which will enlighten you on how your wireless systems are laid out. This is to be done from both the inside and outside of your wireless network. Just like there are third-dimensional images, in wireless networks or systems it is necessary to know how your network is laid out from both inside and outside because wireless networks have a third dimension known as the radio wave dimension. The radio wave dimension makes it possible for your wireless system to be discovered from either side of your physical building or firewall. This dimension is capable of showing you not only external and internal configuration information but also information that is tagged explicitly to the wireless radio waves being transmitted inside and outside of the network.

On a wired network, the process of transmitting data is a bit different compared to that of a wireless network. This is because a wireless network opens a new dimension for its process. As mentioned earlier, these radio waves can be seen on a virtual third dimension; in effect, this dimension gives hackers a kind of accessibility to be able to jump over a conventional boundary.

Below are the best available tools for mapping your network perfectly and professionally.

- **Network Stumbler:** With years of research, we can say that this is the best tool for mapping your wireless network APs both internally and externally. You can download this tool from **www.netstumbler.com/downloads**. Network Stumbler is a Windows OS-based tool. This tool or software allows you to scan the airwaves from outside your building. It will give you an analysis report about what a hacker sitting in the park or driving by can see on your network. You can also run this software from the inside to help you find any additional wireless APs that don't belong.

- **AiroPeek:** This is another fantastic tool that can help you gather network map information. It is also known as a Wireless Network Analyser and/or the sniffer.

- **Cheops-ng and QualysGuard:** To start, you will need to gather all the information transmitted through radio frequency (RF) along with any other information regarding the wireless network that is accessible through the internal wired network. To gather this information, you need the open source tool Cheops-ng (at **www.cheops-ng.sourceforge.net**). You can also get the commercial version of QualysGuard at **www.qualys.com**. To create the internal mapping of your wireless network, either of these two tools can help you by laying out general IP addressing structures and internal hostnames. Furthermore, you can perform the same process used internally to map your wireless network outside to determine the external IP addresses and names, along with the DNS hostnames (domain name system) of the public hosts that are available. In short, these two methods can make your wireless network more secure by giving the network more of a backbone.

- **nmap and fping:** In a Windows command prompt, for you to confirm that you are connected to the internet, you can simply type "ping + web address." The web address can be any site, (e.g., **www.Google.com**). If after typing this command you get a statistics report showing the sent packets and other details, you can say that your system is connected to the internet. The same logic applies to the "nmap and fping" here, but this time you actually use the internet. The two of them are considered to be network mapping utilities that allow the usage of the ICMP (Internet Control Message Protocol) to determine the systems that are "alive" and "active" on your network. You can perform this operation by "pinging" a sweep of your network, which can be performed by using the nmap utility (www.insecure.org/nmap). Nmap is a Windows-based utility and the fping utility applies to the UNIX and LINUX operating systems (**www.fping.com**). Although these two utilities will not create a graphical layout view for your network, you should be expecting these sorts of things from network-mapping programs. At the same time, they are very beneficial and useful.

Helpful Tip: It may not be effortless and straightforward to scan your network from the outside, i.e., from the public internet. However, here is what you can do. Try to get any available public IP address that you can assign to your computer for testing. Then, plug in on the "public" side of your router or firewall that is connected openly to the internet.

Additionally, not all of the methods mentioned above will be able to decipher the exact live systems that are wired and the ones which are wireless. You are the one who will determine the IP addresses, IP networks and hostnames belonging to your network or devices. Now that you can map your network successfully and are able to determine the systems that are live and active on your network, the next thing to know is how to scan your wireless network or systems for more information, such as hostnames, open ports and much more.

METHODOLOGY 3: SCANNING YOUR SYSTEMS

By now, your understanding of the wireless network will be broader than what you had before you read this book. You now know more about IP addresses and SSIDs. You can learn more about these two terms through a process called enumeration. The term enumeration can be explained as a form of analyzing everything about your network or system. You create a list of all the details you encountered or discovered in the process, including how they work and what they do. With enumeration, you can find:

- RF signal strength

- Whether ports are open and active on wireless APs and clients

- Whether or not WEP encryption is enabled

- Live wireless hosts

The Network Stumbler network mapping tool mentioned earlier is not only capable of finding live wireless hosts (ad-Hoc clients and APs), it is also designed in such a way that it has the ability to grab more in-depth information regarding Radio Frequency strength and whether or not WEP encryption is enabled. Don't be surprised if you are told that this Network Stumbler tool is also perfect for enumeration.

Port scanners such as SuperScan or nmap are also very good for prodding a network when you are looking to find the network ports that are open on your wireless clients and APs. You can get a more details when you use these tools. You can get access to SuperScan at:

www.foundstone.com/resources/proddesc/superscan.htm

Some developers add a few restrictions to their software, so make sure you check your software licenses, regardless of whether you are using free software. This is to make sure you are abiding by their rules. Much of the software available for free on the internet has a license that says the software cannot be used for commercial purposes. Moreover, if you are using tools with such licenses, you can use them for your personal internal testing; that is still okay. However, if you are testing wireless networks for paying clients, this is like a Bermuda

Triangle you are crossing because you are already going against the license limitation.

Scanning your ports is apparently not just about waiting to get a scan result after the tool has done the scanning. It actually helps you create an even more detailed picture of what is available on your wireless network. It's no wonder that hackers love this. When your ports are scanned, the hackers are given a lot of sensitive information they need to exploit your potential network or system's vulnerabilities. Below is a table of the ports that are vulnerable to attack when opened:

Port	Service	Protocols
20	FTP data	TCP
21	FTP control	TCP
22	SSH	TCP
23	Telnet	TCP
25	Simple Mail Transfer Protocol (SMTP)	TCP
53	Domain Name Office (DNS)	UDP
80	Hypertext Transfer Protocol (HTTP)	TCP
110	Post Office Protocol Version 3 (POP3)	TCP
135	RCP/DCE end point mapper for Microsoft networks	UDP, TCP
137, 138, 139	NetBIOS over TCP/IP	UDP, TCP
161	Simple Network Management Protocol (SNMP)	UDP, TCP
443	HTTPS (HTTP over SSL)	TCP

512, 513, 514 Berkeley r commands	
(e.g., rsh, rlogin and rexec)	TCP
1433 Microsoft SQL server	UDP, TCP
1434 Microsoft SQL monitor	UDP, TCP
3389 Windows terminal server	TCP

METHODOLOGY 4: DETERMINE THE SERVICES THAT ARE RUNNING

You need to be more careful when you are scanning your system's or network's ports because, during the process, there is a possibility that your system's details will be snagged. Remember that knowledge is power. The knowledge can be used to help you or harm you. However, if you as a person are capable of determining the open ports of your wireless network, somebody who isn't you is capable of determining those open ports as well. Connecting to the open ports you have available can give you more insight into enumeration information like:

- The software and its firmware version (it will be returned as an error or banner message)

- Acceptable usage policy warnings on banner pages

- Acceptable usage login warnings

- The configurations of your OS and applications

- Your OS versions (it will be returned as an error or banner message)

During the process of connecting to your open ports, there is a probability that you will discover some vulnerabilities or a ton of exploitable information about your APs, servers and workstations. Do not be afraid at this point because most of your wireless system is likely not public facing, so the possibility that your wireless devices have public IP addresses is very low. On the other hand, you need some wireless-based servers or wireless hotspots you must enable to be publicly accessible. These systems are usually and easily reachable by an attacker because even your firewalls and other protective measures might not stop them. When an attacker has access to it, obtaining your configuration details will be very easy. The accessibility will also cause some unavoidable vulnerability, which is a necessary evil if you want your network to do actual, useful work.

Nevertheless, all information obtained can be used against you. Keep in mind that "Eternal Vigilance is the price of productivity." This will lead us to perform an actual vulnerability test through which you can discover the true vulnerabilities in your network. Although the result of the test can be a false positive, the issues it produces won't matter.

METHODOLOGY 5: FIND AND LOCATE SPECIFIC VULNERABILITIES

Now you've found potential windows into your wireless network. Now is the time to find out whether there are any significant vulnerabilities you should be mindful of. Try to see what your hacker might see. How is this done? You will have to connect to your wireless systems and make a systematic, discreet attempt to see what you can find from a hacker's point of view. When you perform this process, you are likely to locate and gather more crucial information and also capture data out of thin air using a sniffer tool. You may even determine whether a specific patch is missing on your network.

Anything found must be counted. Do not discount what you have found because you are just getting to the formal

"Vulnerability Assessment" portion of your testing. Regardless of whether or not you are going deeper or prodding your wireless network further, the information you already discovered may contain some juicy vulnerabilities like WEP not being enabled and default SSIDs. Furthermore, some critical servers are accessible through a wireless network. These vulnerabilities can be looked at in two ways: manually or automatically.

MANUAL ASSESSMENT

This is the first method you can employ to look at these vulnerabilities. It's also the most time consuming, although it is essential. At first, using this method to assess weaknesses can be difficult but time, dedication and commitment will make it easier later on. This is called a manual assessment, although it involves numerous semiautomatic security tools which don't perform a run-of-the-mill robot assessment because of the need for a guiding hand in the process. Understanding what works and what doesn't will help with your manual assessment. Manually assessing your network's vulnerabilities is necessary, and various other ways through which you can perform this assessment are mentioned later on in this book.

AUTOMATIC ASSESSMENT

This is the second method or way of looking for vulnerabilities in your system or network. You can perform this automated method by using an open source tool called Nessus. (You can get it at www.nessus.org.) You can also use the commercial LANguard Network Security Scanner (**www.gfi.com/lannetscan**) or QualysGuard. These tools have the ability to help you automate the whole process of vulnerability assessment by scanning live systems, determining whether vulnerabilities (either actual or potential) exist. The time taken by these tools is usually a bit lengthy, so while they scan for vulnerabilities, you can catch up on emails or watch a movie. There is no way you can perform an automated ethical hacking without the use of these tools.

Many software choices are available today. Thus, you should be able to explore the internet for better wireless hacking tools which are absolutely free. However, if you have a strong budget, you can go for the premium tools. They all work well at running their own specific tests, although when you are ready to take a closer look at your system's vulnerabilities, these free commercial tools will prove their worth. You will get what you pay for the moment you are delicately probing the operating system and all of the applications that are active on your wireless network.

FINDING MORE INFORMATION

When you have finally used your tools to find the suspected vulnerabilities on your network, you can still take numerous steps to learn more about the vulnerabilities and resources. Doing this will give you more information about the weaknesses you have gathered. The right place for you to start is at your wireless vendor's website. For instance, if you are using a Windows operating system and have an issue with it which supersedes your knowledge, a good place to start is the Windows website. On their website, you can look at the users' forums where you can find related problems and solutions. You may even be lucky enough to find available security patches. The database below can also be exploited for a more in-depth idea about a specific vulnerability as well as these fixes:

- NIST ICAT Metabase (located at **http://icat.nist.gov/icat.cfm**)

- US-CERT Vulnerability Notes Database (located at **www.kb.cert.org/vuls**)

- Common Vulnerabilities and Exposures (located at **http://cve.mitre.org/cve**)

Another excellent method you can use to find more information about specific vulnerability problems is using a search engine. It is recommended to use the Google web and groups search for queries. You will likely find a solution and more information about what you are looking for.

METHODOLOGY 6: HACKING INTO THE SYSTEM

This is the last methodology on our list. You should have been able to try the methodologies mentioned earlier. After you map your network, try to see the systems running and find possible vulnerabilities. There is one more phase in the ethical hacking methodology but it is optional. This phase is called the **system penetration phase**. This is the phase that will truly test what information and systems can actually be compromised on your wireless network and provide you with information regarding the top goals of a malicious hacker.

Hacking into your wireless system can be seen as being given unauthorized access to resources and to geting away with the information. This is when you will join the wireless network, connect to different systems and do things like:

- Browsing the Internet

- Logging into the network

- Changing the AP configuration settings

- Sending and receiving e-mails

- Editing, copying and deleting Files

- Mapping to network drives

- Capturing data being sent over the network using a sniffer such as AiroPeek or Ethereal (**www.ethereal.com**)

We can say that these things are unethical, but hackers are doing them. So it makes sense for you to try them yourself and get insight into what is possible on your network.

Helpful Tip: When you are hacking or penetrating your system, be very careful and penetrate with caution. Take your time; don't be in a rush to damage anything or take steps that might get you lost. In other words, you want to minimize any disruptions you might create.

CHAPTER FOUR: TEN BEST TOOLS FOR HACKING WIRELESS NETWORKS

For any job to be done in the right way, you need the right tool for it. Following are the 10 best tools for performing your hack:

TOOL 1:   LAPTOP COMPUTER

Before you can surf the internet, you need an internet data connection. The root of everything you can perform on the internet is a computer system. Without a computer system, there is nothing you can do. For beginners, you need a computer to conduct your tests; I recommend portable systems such as laptops. While it is possible to hack using a pocket personal computer (PC), it has limited tools compared to what you'll find on a laptop.

Different wireless network systems have different specifications, so you should use a system that has multiple operating capabilities. Use a system that can dual boot Windows and Linux, or preferably a Windows-based system that is running a VM (virtual machine) program such as VMware on which you can install two different Operating Software. Most computer systems that are capable only of running a single operating system always have minimal hardware requirements.

In terms of specifications, the least you should be looking for on a single operating system is RAM of at least 256MB, a Pentium III processor and at least 30-40 HDD (hard disk drive). However, if you intend to run a VMware or any other kind of virtual machine system on your system, you might want to look elsewhere for a better specification. You will need more RAM and a more powerful hard drive.

TOOL 2:   WIRELESS NETWORK CARD

Getting a laptop with the specifications of your choice is the first step. Now you have a laptop and you need an efficient wireless NIC (network interface card). Find a PC NIC that is not only compatible with various wireless tools but also one that is compatible with an external antenna. This compatibility will help you pick up more signals efficiently. Everything today is usually built on class, which means that we can have devices that are built according to our budgets. Some devices are available for people with low budgets while others exist for people with higher budgets. Most of the wireless NICs in today's laptops are good general-purpose cards even though you can limit your test results. This is true because they have a shorter radio range capability than internal antennas.

TOOL 3:   ANTENNAS AND CONNECTING CABLES

There are different types of antennas, all of which have different signal ranges. Take, for instance, a high-gain omnidirectional or unidirectional antenna that will perform wonders in the process of your scanning airwaves for wireless systems. A cantenna is another option. When buying an antenna, go for one that has a pigtail connection matching the one on your wireless NIC. Note that the length of these pigtail cables should not be too long, so keep them as short as possible. This is because these pigtails are made with a critically thin microwave coax; the cables have impartially high signal losses at microwave frequencies and also with the connectors that are placed on either end of the cable. To avoid this stress, make sure your pigtail cable is no longer than five feet, which will help you avoid high cable losses.

TOOL 4:   GPS RECEIVER

According to its dictionary meaning, a global positioning satellite (GPS) is an audio-visual device that can be fitted into a civilian's road vehicle as an aid for navigation. If you'll be warwalking or wardriving, or if your wireless system spans a large building, this is the perfect time to think along a new global dimension. GPS will come in handy in these situations because you'll have the ability to integrate your wireless testing tool or software, which will pinpoint the exact locations of wireless systems within a few meters. GPS is the tool used by spies in movies to track their targets even though anyone can use it as needed.

TOOL 5:   STUMBLING SOFTWARE

The stumbling tool is essential to the hacking profession and you can't do without it. A stumbling software will help you map out things like signal strength, SSIDs and the systems that use WEP encryptions. There are many kinds of software you can use to perform this type of operation, but it is recommended to use the Network Stumbler if you are on Windows. You can also use a Wireless NIC management software. Did you know you can even perform stumble using the management software built into Windows XP? You can, although it's applicable only for basic stumbling.

TOOL 6:   WIRELESS NETWORK ANALYZER

So now you've been able to stumble the network successfully. It doesn't end there for you as a hacker. You need to probe deep into the airwaves. You can get this done by using a network analyzer software. Programs such as AiroPeek, Kismet and Ethereal can help you analyze and monitor wireless channels for protocols that are in use. These tools can also help you search for wireless system anomalies. The best part about them is that they can even capture wireless data, right out of thin air.

TOOL 7: PORT SCANNER

Port scanning is also an essential step that needs to be completed when hacking a wireless network like a pro. The best tools to use are nmap or SuperScan. They are considered great tools for scanning the wireless system that you stumbled to help find more in-depth information about what's running. Moreover, they are useful because they will help you find what's potentially vulnerable in the network.

TOOL 8: VULNERABILITY ASSESSMENT TOOL

Probing that network further to see the vulnerabilities that still exist in the network is another great step to take. The best tools for this task are LANguard Network Security Scanner, Nessus or QualysGuard. When the scan is run using either of these tools and you have a result indicating what is still vulnerable on your network, the information you obtain can also be used as a form of protection that reveals where hackers can potentially exploit your network.

TOOL 9: GOOGLE

You can go to google and run a quick search on the previously mentioned tools, which will provide more interesting results. You can use Google to search for Network Stumbler and NSI files, dig deeper into web server software built into your AP, research specific vulnerabilities, find the latest wireless security tools and learn about new hacking tricks.

TOOL 10: 802.11 REFERENCE GUIDE/BOOK

You will not remember everything you read. Even experts need to continue learning. So while you are carrying out your ethical hacking on a wireless network, you will need a good reference book or guide on IEEE 802.11 standards. This standard is very complex and evolves over time, which means you'll want to continue reading about the latest trends. You'll likely need to look up information about channel frequency ranges, what a certain packet does and what it is used for. Perhaps, you may also need to learn more about a specific default 802.11 setting.

CHAPTER FIVE: CRACKING ENCRYPTION

Chapter Objectives:

- ✓ **UNDERSTANDING ENCRYPTION**
- ✓ **THE ENCRYPTING FRAMES**
- ✓ **WEP PROBLEMS**
- ✓ **UPGRADING TO WPA**
- ✓ **THE CONCEPT OF AES ENCRYPTION**
- ✓ **TUNNELLING THE INTERNET WITH A VPN**

Most people believe that when something is encrypted, it is unbreakable and secure, but this is not true. As technology keeps progressing and new security features regarding encryption may not be as robust as you like. Did you know that cryptography features can have flaws? You may use the wrong algorithm for the right task, a short key, a flawed algorithm or even a security breach. In this chapter, we will discuss how one or all of these flaws can affect your wireless networks. The techniques you need to use to strengthen your access point will be discussed in this chapter.

Helpful Tip: It is recommended that you employ the built-in security features as your important overall defense mechanism.

<u>**WHAT CAN HAPPEN**</u>

One of the features of the IEEE 802.11 standard is that a wireless network must maintain a secure working environment. One primary feature was the adoption of encryption to provide the following:

- **Message Privacy:** Encryption is interesting in the sense that you can be sure that your encrypted sensitive information is safe while it is being sent between two wireless entities. This is the case because it will prevent the third party from tracking your data. Therefore, your privacy is guaranteed to a certain extent.

- **Message Integrity:** An entity can help both the sender and receiver know if someone has changed or accessed the message being sent.

Just like any other technology, there will be some shortcomings. Despite the fact that 802.11 standards attempted to address integrity and privacy, some things still never fell into place. Below is a discussion of these features and their drawbacks.

PROTECTING MESSAGE PRIVACY

It is not possible for you to design a system without considering its security level; you don't want your system vulnerable to attack. IEEE 802.11 tried to support users that had their own privacy with the use of cryptographic procedures, which address the wireless user interface. When these techniques were introduced, the first and most widely used algorithm was called *wired equivalent privacy*. WEP was discussed in the previous chapters and is one of the first algorithms to be made to ensure privacy.

Wired equivalent privacy uses an RC4 symmetric key which is incorporated into a stream cipher system to produce a pseudo-random data structure. The WEP keystream has a simple function that is added via a *modulo two calculation* to the data being transmitted. One may say, "Wow, WEP is so secure." Actually, it's really not. Unfortunately, all of its attributes don't add up to very impressive security.

It is a simple algorithm–the longer an encryption, the harder it is to crack it. WEP is a bit outdated because it supports only the

40-bit size of the shared key, as defined in the 802.11 standards. However, most of the vendors in the market are offering non-standard extensions of WEP which support key lengths from 40 to about 104 bits. It should be noted that WEP uses IV to seed its algorithm before it encrypts the frame.

It is generally known in the wireless hacking industry that an increase in key size will have an increased effect on the security of a cryptographic technique. Therefore, if you have a flawed implementation or design, it can prevent you from having a long key.

According to research, it can be concluded that keys longer than 80 bits make brute force cryptanalysis a nearly impossible task for smooth and robust design and implementation. However, most 802.11 WLAN keys rely on scrawny, which is 40 bits. However, no computer is completely safe. In recent attacks, it was shown that the WEP approach to privacy is very vulnerable to some attacks. These attacks were successful regardless of the key size.

PROTECTING MESSAGE INTEGRITY

Unlike picking up your phone to call your friend or to share sensitive information, it's not safe because the third party can breach your communication. Encrypting your messages prevents you from having total flexibility regarding the messages being sent because you can be sure your information is 100 percent secure. Encryption's basic security task involves making sure your messages get to the receiver intact. The IEEE 802.11 specification offers good security in this respect by outlining a simple check called CRC (*Cyclic Redundancy Check*). The purpose of this check is to ensure your messages are provided with data integrity, making your transmitted messages between clients and access points more secure.

This security service was made to reject any message anyone may have changed during the transmission. This service does not mean that you can simply log into your network, compose a message to a client and assume total security. It needs a lot more. The access point and client compute a CRC-32 frame check sequence called an ICV (*Integrity Check Value*) for each frame before transmission. Encryption isn't a direct message you can send to a friend to read in pure English or Chinese. (You can call it tech jargon.) It actually won't make any sense to a layman who happens to read an encrypted message.

Despite the fact that a message is encrypted, there must be a way for the receiver to read and understand it in a human-readable language. The process of reading encrypted data or information is called decryption. To confirm whether the message being transmitted hasn't been changed, the receiver will need to decrypt the frame and then recompute the CRC on the message. After the decryption, the receiver will compare the computed CRC with the original message. In this process, if the receiver sees that the CRCs are not equal, it can be deduced that an error has occurred. At this point, the receiver will have to discard the frame since it has been compromised.

This is a great idea. If you think this form of encrypting information is the best, think again. This idea is poorly implemented, as it is possible to flip bits with data that will still end up passing the CRC check.

Verdict: Message modification is possible.

With all of the pros of CRC encryption, one would think that it is a top-notch security feature. However, it is possible to modify a message that is sent on CRC, which has made the CRC-32 inadequate for protecting against intentional data integrity attacks. Therefore, you need more real cryptographic mechanisms such as a message digest or MAC (message authentication code) to prevent deliberate attacks. Imagine trying to hack the network of a company like Facebook, and your only tool is Internet Explorer. Does this even make sense? Remember, you need the right tools for the right job. Using non-cryptographic mechanisms will facilitate an attack against cryptography. One reason for this is the use of 64 or 128 keys for privacy and integrity. Thus, this is a cryptography no-no.

USING ENCRYPTION

Blogs, the press and other online articles have done a lot to discourage both individuals and organizations from using wireless networks. If you have been paying attention to the tech blogs, you will have seen a lot of negative articles regarding the security of wireless networks. The focus of the negativity lies with those dealing with encryption. However, not everyone posting on the internet understands what they are posting about; some just copy and paste, while others are paid to post. Research shows that most people who post negative articles about wireless security do not have a clear understanding of the basis of WEP. Through the name WEP (Wired Equivalent Privacy), the developers intended to give users the same level of security that is found on a wired network. However, to be candid, this level does not provide much security at all. With the exclusion of a fully switched environment, eavesdroppers can have their way with frames while traversing a wired network. The implementation and design of WEP were actually never intended to provide message integrity or confidentiality in any form.

In the design of WEP, there is an incorporation of a symmetrical Ron's code four algorithm (RC4) and a Pseudo Random Number Generator (PRNG). The initial implementation of WEP uses a standard which specified 40 and 128-bit key lengths with a 24-bit IV (Initialisation Vector). One of the issues it encountered was incomplete coverage of network layers: WEP encrypts layers 3 through 7, although it doesn't encrypt the MAC layer, which is layer 2. Recall that WEP uses a symmetrical algorithm; this is why WEP gives its clients the key and any other necessary configuration data.

RC4 configuration, in general, isn't so bad because it is used in most web browsers for their SSL (Secure Sockets Layer). However, the problem it has with WEP implementation and also the negative sense of security it creates is not so good. However, how does this work exactly in WEP?

The simple algorithm it uses works in such a way that it takes the initialization vector, which is originally in a plaintext (human readable) form. After taking it in IV form, it sticks it on the front end of the secret key. (The decrypter will actually know this.) When this is done, WEP will take the result and plug it into the RC4 to regenerate a fresh key stream. The algorithm will then XORs the key stream with the inbuilt tool called CipherText. This will give us the values in plaintext. Finally, WEP re-performs the CRC-32 checksum on the transmitted message to ensure that it matches the integrity check value exactly as it is on the encrypted plaintext. What if the checksums did not match each other? WEP will immediately assume someone else somewhere has compromised the packets being sent and will automatically discard it.

Earlier, access points were mentioned. Access points generally have only three encryption settings available. These are:

None: The name looks simple, but these access point encryption settings happen to be the riskiest of them all. The reason is that the data being transmitted can easily be intercepted by someone else, who can read and even alter the unencrypted data traversing the network. You must be careful using these settings.

40-Bit Shared Key: The increase in bits doesn't actually say it has its own bad side. This setting will encrypt the network communication data, but can still be compromised; it is just a bit safer than the first settings. However, on the bright side, this 40-bit encryption has been broken before using a brute force cryptanalysis attack, which was commenced on a high-end graphics computer. It should be noted that it is also possible to break the keys on a low-end computer. By the end, the 40-bit shared key has a questionable value. Later in this book, we will talk about the tools you can use to recover 40-bit keys. However, if it is possible for you to recover such keys, it is possible for other hackers to achieve the same goal.

104-bit settings: The higher the number of encryption keys, the harder it will be for another hacker to crack them. This setting is considered more reliable, safer and at least more secure than 40-bit encryption because it simply has more significant differences in terms of the size of the cryptographic key space. It is sometimes also referred to as a 128-bit setting. However, poor cryptographic design in the use of initialization vectors has made it not so true for 802.11 WEP. It is recommended as a good practice simply because it is still more secure. Whenever you are purchasing anything from any vendor, be vigilant. Check on upgrades for software and firmware. You might get lucky and find some that solve a few of the WEP problems.

If you are lucky enough, you will find some vendors who support 152-bit keys, but this is just an example. It is generalized that 40-bit keys are not competent enough for a regular system's form of encryption. For you to be confident in your security, the least you should be looking for is an 80-bit key. Research has shown that encryption keys longer than 80 bits actually get the job done better. The longer your keys, the lesser the chance a third party has to compromise your access point by using a brute force attack. In short, this setting is considered more secure, so go for it.

WEP WEAKNESSES

All computer wireless networks have weaknesses. Researchers have examined the security issues of a WLAN that uses WEP and documented the attacks that are carried out by malicious hackers. The problems are mentioned below.

- **Passive attacks:** Problems based on this level are statistical analysis issues that are used to decrypt traffic.

- **Active attacks:** These kinds of attacks are based on tricking the AP (access point) in order to decrypt traffic.

- **Active attacks used to inject new traffic from authorized mobile stations:** These attacks are concerned with known plaintexts.

- **Dictionary attacks:** These are attacks that are carried out after analysing sufficient traffic on a very busy network or server.

Having a lazy bodyguard guarding your house is apparently still better than having no one. One of the biggest issues WEP is facing arises when an installer fails to allow it to perform properly in the first place. Having security that is not good enough is better than having none at all.

Don't forget that even your car needs regular service so that it won't break down. The point is to make sure you are changing your WEP keys periodically. Otherwise, consider the example of a car that is not being serviced regularly–it will be prone to failure. If there are too many users in your wireless network who are sharing almost the same keys for long periods of time, then this will cause your system to be more vulnerable. Other hackers can easily capture all of the frames that are needed to crack your keys if you do not change your keys often enough.

However, we can't place all of the blame on the AP administrators for not regularly changing keys. The reason is that the WEP protocols themselves don't offer any sort of key managing provisions. This situation is critically dangerous. Take, for instance, someone working in your organization who lost his/her laptop; the password can be compromised. And that's not the only bad news; it can be compromised with other computers that are using the same password.

There is a reason why everyone in the world can't be rich: If everyone were rich, money would no longer have value. The logic here is that shared keys could compromise your wireless network. When the number of users sharing your key grows, so do your chances of putting your wireless network at risk. Cryptography has a simple tenet, which is that "the security of a particular computer is generally reliant on the privacy of the keys." The moment you expose your keys, you have exposed the text. The moment you share or expose the key, you have given a cracker the access to decipher it. Plus, if most of the stations share an identical key, you can be sure you have given an eavesdropper access to control a huge sum of your traffic for analytic attacks.

Helpful Tips:

1. Keep your keys private.

2. Don't share your key with anyone you don't trust.

3. Periodically change your keys.

4. Always have a backup of your security files.

5. Use longer keys for your access point encryptions.

ATTACKING WEP

Attacking WEP might be so simple that a layman could do it, but we have examined the best ways for you to achieve this easily. There are several passive and active ways to attack WEP. They are:

- Active attacks are used to inject traffic based on known plaintexts.

- Active attacks are used to decrypt traffic by tricking access points.

- Dictionary-based attacks are carried out after enough traffic is gathered.

- Passive attacks are used to decrypt traffic through statistical analysis.

Below is a description of these attacks in more detail.

1. ACTIVE TRAFFIC INJECTION

Assume that a malicious hacker knows the plaintext version you used in a specific message that was encrypted using the passive technique. The bad news about knowing your plaintext version is that he or she can use this information to construct new and correctly encrypted packets on your network. After construction, you should expect him or her to insert these packets on your network. However, for the hacker to achieve this, he or she will have to construct a new message by calculating CRC-32 values and performing some sort of bit-flips on the original message in its encrypted form. After achieving this, the attacker can send the packets to the access points completely undetected. The good news is that there are several variations of a technique you can use to avoid such an attack.

- **AirePlay:** This is an interesting tool that you must have. This program allows you to take any captured packet and then reinject it back into your network.

- **WEPWedgie:** You can also use this tool for injecting frames but it's a little different. The WEPWedgie toolkit can be used to determine 802.11 WEP keystreams and also to inject traffic with known keystreams. (Download the toolkit at **http://sourceforge.net/projects/wepwedgie.**)

2. ACTIVE ATTACK FROM BOTH SIDES

This is an extension of the active injection technique which was mentioned in the previous section. The role of the attacker in this section is simple; the hacker makes random guesses about the packet header contents instead of the packet payload. Bit-flipping was mentioned in the previous section, but we didn't explain what it actually does. Bit-flipping can transform the destination address and then route traffic to dangerous devices where transmission can occur. By employing educated guessing, the attacker has what it takes to get your port information and then allow passage through firewalls by changing it to the default port for web traffic, which is port 80.

3. TABLE-BASED ATTACK

Encryption tables are built from the high likelihood that some information about WEP initialization vectors (IVs) will be reused at short intervals. With the use of a passive technique, the hacker can gain some plaintext information. When the hacker finally gains this information, he or she can then compute the RC4 keystream, which is used by the initialization vector. Research has shown that repetitive techniques usually allow an attacker to build a complete decryption table based on all possible IVs. The bad news is that it gives the hacker an edge in deciphering every packet that is transmitted.

4. PASSIVE ATTACK DECRYPTION

If you are looking for the definition of an intrusion, this is it. The attacker not only attacks your network but intrudes deeply. The attacker sits in one corner and monitors your traffic until an initialization vector collision occurs. What is a collision? This is a state in which an algorithm reuses an initialization vector. However, your secrets aren't safe in the course of a collision. This is because when a collision occurs, both the shared secret and the repeated initialization vector will result in a keystream that has been used previously. Moreover, when an algorithm sends out information, it will send it in a ciphertext. Then, a hacker who is keeping track of all the traffic going in and out will be able to identify when a collision occurs. When this happens, the hacker will be able to use the resulting XOR information to infuse the data regarding the message content.

Naturally, IP traffic is very much redundant. Therefore, replication of the process can easily yield enough information to decipher the encrypted message.

CRACKING KEYS

Anything that uses an algorithm can be cracked; it just depends on how flexible you are with your cracking skills. So far in this book, we have extensively discussed WEP and its flaws. The wired equivalent protocol is just an algorithm that is generally used to protect wireless networks from easy attacks. Unfortunately, this security feature has a lot of security flaws, which make WEP very much open to crack attacks. The following things are needed before someone can crack WEP keys.

- A large number of captured frames.

- A program that can process the frames that were captured.

Numerous tools on the internet can crack WEP keys; some are free while some are paid. For now, we will focus on tools such as WEPcrack and AirSnort to crack keys, although you can use any tool that does the job. You can use a program like Kismet, which can save weak initialization vectors (IVs) to feed into another cracking program like WEPcrack.

USING WEPCRACK

This tool is considered to be one of the most famous tools for cracking WEP keys. WEPcrack (download at http://sourceforge.net/projects/wepcrack) was the first WEP cracking tool to go public. This amazing tool can capture logs and crack IVs to provide important keys. However, before you can run WEPcrack, you will need some PERL and packets.

The developers of this tool have coded it in such a way that it can be used anywhere there is an interpreter for PERL. Moreover, this requirement is easy to meet for UNIX platform users. For you to run WEPcrack in UNIX, just run the command wizard, type the code "per1/tmp/WEPcrack.pl." However, if your installed location is different, simply change the "per1" to the name of the folder where you installed the WEPcrack script. Microsoft does not provide PERL. This might be astonishing for Windows users, as it won't be so easy to use WEPcrack. However, the best alternative for Windows users is a tool called Cygwin. You can get it online or perhaps you can get a PERL interpreter for your Windows operating system instead, such as a tool called ActivePerl.

Let's assume you are on the Windows OS and you decide to get ActivePerl and install it. You can download it at **www.activestate.com/Products/ActivePerl**. With ActivePerl, you can achieve the same goal as a UNIX user on your Windows platform. To install this tool and use it to run WEPcrack, simply follow the steps below:

1. Download the tool from the ActiveState website using the link above.

2. Start the **ActivePerl setup**.

3. The license agreement will appear on the screen. Read it and then accept by clicking **Next**.

4. A new window will appear on the screen asking you to choose where you want the ActivePerl to be installed. Choose your location; then click on **Next**.

5. Step (IV) above is optional; you can choose to install it in a custom directory if you don't want it to be installed in the root directory. To install in a custom directory, click on the **Browse button** and then browse the directory trees on your hard drive until you see the location where you want it to be installed.

6. The new window that pops up will be a **PPM New Features window**. You can either give it access to send your profile details to ASPN by clicking on **enable PPM3**, or just click **Next** and ignore.

7. Based on your choice, any option you think you won't be using can be ignored by clicking on **Next**.

8. Here, click on the **Install Button** to install ActivePerl on your Windows computer.

9. Step (VII) can take a little while to complete. It will give you an installation status window where you can see the progress of the installation. After this process is complete, you are ready to use PERL.

10. Select **Run** from the start menu.

11. Type *command* in the dialog box and click **OK**.

12. Launch your command prompt by pressing **Win+R**; then type **cmd** in the dialog box and press **enter** on your keyboard. When the command prompt opens, type **perl\progra~1\wepcrack\pcapgetIV.pl**.

13. The path in step (X) is the default root where the tool should be installed and located. If you have used a custom directory during the installation process, make sure you edit the directories in the command so that it can work properly. However, the Perl routine we show here is just an example. The script itself is useless because for it to function properly, you need a captured packet that you can drop in from another program, for instance, **prismdump** or **ethereal**. A large number of frames (like 5 million) will be needed. After this, you can proceed to the next step.

14. Start the WEPcrack software by typing **perl\progra~1\wepcrack\wepcrack. pl ivfile.log**.

15. When you are done, you can close the window by clicking on the X at the upper right corner.

16. Take note that the key is always in a decimal format. Therefore, you will still need to convert the decimal into a hexadecimal format before you can use it successfully.

USING AIRSNORT

This is another amazing passive scanner tool used for cracking WEP keys. This tool works in a very simple and interesting way. It gathers weak IVs and begins to crack the WEP key. The closest approximation to the total initialization vectors that could be in a key is 16 million. In these 16 million initialization vectors, there are approximately 9,000 128-bit keys that are stupendously weak. AirSnort will then scan all 16 million keys and look for the weak ones. Members of the Shmoo Group estimated the number of weak IVs needed to determine the WEP key and concluded that there were approximately 2,000 weak initialization vectors.

The AirSnort software can be downloaded at **http://sourceforge.net/projects/airsnort/**.

AirSnort runs smoothly on the UNIX platform. It can also be used on Windows. To run AirSnort on Windows, you will need to download WinAirSnort at **www.nwp.nevillon.org/attack.html/**.

You can use this tool on Linux as well. Follow the steps below to install AirSnort on Linux:

1. Download the file and unzip it. To unzip it on Linux, use the command below:

   /#gunzip airsnort-0.2.7e.tar.gz

2. At this point, you will have to Untar the file. To achieve this, use the command below:

   /#tar −xvf airsnort-0.2.7e.tar

3. During the process of uncompressing the file, change the directory to the location you used. You can do this by using the command below:

   /#cd airsnort-0.2.7e

4. Compile and install AirSnort.

5. Don't forget that Linux platforms differ from each other. Most of them require different commands to work with them. During the process of compilation, the binaries of AirSnort will be placed in the directory **/user/ local/bin**. But this command varies because your

platform might be different. If the command doesn't work for your Linux platform, try one of the following:

/airsnort-0.2.7e# make
/airsnort-0.2.7e# ./autogen.sh
/airsnort-0.2.7e# make install

6. After the installation, to run the AirSnort software, open your terminal window and input the command below:

/airsnort-0.2.7e# airsnort

7. To select the channels, use the up and down arrows to select the channels you want to scan.

8. Recall that you can use Kismet to scan your wireless network. Preferably, you can use any tool of your choice. If you used Kismet to scan your wireless network to identify channels, it can be deduced that you know the channels you want to monitor. However, if you wish to monitor all the channels, click the **Scan** button.

9. Select your network device from the network device drop-down list.

10. You will manually select the network device you want to use. The device selected will be the device which you want to monitor. For instance, select eth0. AirSnort will not put the cards into monitoring automatically, but rather it will do this manually.

11. To select your network card manually, click on the **Card Type** drop-down list. Then select your preferred wireless network interface card (NIC).

12. For instance, select ORiNOCO.

13. You can control the time it takes to crack the key. For instance, if you wish to decrease the time it will take to

crack the key, increase the 40-bit or 128-bit crack breadth.

14. Note that increasing the crack breadth will increase the number of key possibilities that can be examined when AirSnort attempts to break the WEP key.

15. Start the cracking process by clicking on the start button on the lower left part of the bar at the bottom.

16. When the process begins, AirSnort will start showing you sensitive SSIDs and eventually crack the key for you.

USING AIRCRACK

Christophe Devine developed this WEP cracking tool. You can download it at **www.cro.net:8040/code/network**. Aircrack was designed to work effectively on the two operating systems, which are Linux and Windows. For the sake of this tutorial, we will concentrate more on the version of Aircrack specially designed for the Windows OS.

Aircrack is considered to be one of the fastest means of attacking WEP. It implements KoreK's attacks along with the improved Fluhrer-Mantin-Shamir (FMS). To perform an effective hack with Aircrack, all you need to do is collect as many packets as you can from a WEP encrypted wireless network. Aircrack uses packets to carry out its tweak. Follow the steps below to use Aircrack:

1. Access the website above to download the Aircrack software **aircrack-2.1.zip**. After downloading it successfully, use an unzipping tool to unzip the Aircrack file. You can use **Winrar** to unzip. After the zipped file has been unzipped, in the list of the inner files, you should now see a file named **airodump** in the **win32** subdirectory. This airodump program is the packet-capture tool.

2. To start the packet capture, simply double click on the **airodump** icon. A new window will pop up with a list of known wireless interfaces. Choose the one to use by selecting it and hitting the enter key. A new window should pop up again. In this new window, choose your interface and press the enter key. For instance, to choose Orinoco/Realtek interfaces, choose **o,** or if you would like to go for the Aironet/Atheros interface, choose **a.**

3. Now enter the channel you want to scan and then press the enter key. If you happen to know the number of the channel you want to wardrive, enter its number manually. If you don't know the number of the channel, enter the number zero (**0**) and scan all of the available channels.

4. Give a name you want for the output file and hit the enter key. Make sure you enter a proper name that makes sense here. You also want to make sure you give a date and time to the name you will be using.

5. You will have many MAC address options proportional to the available channels. If you wish to filter a specific MAC address, enter it manually. However, if not, just enter the letter **p**, which stands for none. Then press the enter key.

6. Anticipate and observe as the Airodump starts capturing frames. A new window will appear as the operation proceeds. From this new window, you can see the progress and status of the Airodump while it racks up on initialisation vectors.

7. Double click on the Aircrack icon.

8. Another awesome attribute about Aircrack is that it can determine a WEP key in few seconds, although the execution time varies. It took John many days to crack a

WEP with less activity and a 40-bit key. Note that shorter execution times will require more traffic, more luck, even more initialization vectors and the lowest successful **fudge factor**. This factor is a setting that tells Aircrack how wildly and deeply it should guess when it's trying out new keys. Aircrack was designed in such a way that the higher the fudge factor, the higher the keys Aircrack will try. This rule will increase both the likelihood of the attack working out well and the potential time of execution.

9. This fudge factor has its default value, which is 2 (two), but you have the chance to set it to your own custom positive integer value. However, try to change the default value of the fudge factor only when other means of attack do not succeed. The general trade-off is: The higher the fudge factor, the longer the execution time.

10. If you choose to use a value for the fudge factor that is different from the default value, which is two, type it manually and press the enter key.

11. Access the file you created in steps **1-9**.

12. You can manually type the name and hit the enter key. You can also do it like a pro by dragging the file to the place where you need it.

13. Enter the number **0** and press the enter key.

USING WEPLAB

This is another interesting tool developed by Jose Ignacio Sanchez. You can use this to crack the WEP key. WepLab (**http://weplab.sourceforge.net**) provides an alternative implementation of the KoreK attacks. WepLab is a bit similar to Aircrack's fudge factor. In Aircrack's fudge factor, the default is two while WepLab has a default of 50 percent, which is very aggressive. WepLab also provides a probability adjustment with its percent command, which is a line option (--perc). WepLab operates in relatively few branches–that is, higher settings increase the number of branches taken. Another advantage for using WepLab is that it provides brute force attack and dictionary cracking attacks, which can be very useful in cracking WEP keys. These attributes are the things that make WepLab an essential tool in the industry.

FINDING OTHER TOOLS

The ability to conduct more research on your own is the first step in learning more about this field. Search engines will come in handy in this section. There are thousands (if not millions) of tools available on the internet that you can find only when you conduct your research. Nevertheless, you are not totally stranded. Below are other tools that you can use to crack WEP keys:

- ChopChop: You can access it at **www.netstumbler.org/showthread.php?t=12489**

- Auditor Security Collector: Access it at **http://remote-exploit.org/?page=auditor**

- Jc-wepcracker: **www.astalavista.com/?section=dir&cmd=file&id =3316**

- Dwepcrack: **www.e.kth.se/~pvz/wifi/**

- WepAttack: **http://wepattack.sourceforge.net/**

You can check out this page for an excellent comparison of the tools: **www.securityfocus.com/infocus/1814**.

COUNTERMEASURES AGAINST HOME NETWORK-ENCRYPTION ATTACKS

There are some things you can still do to protect yourself from attacks, even at home. They are:

- Rotate the keys

- Use Wi-Fi Protected Access (WPA)

ROTATING KEYS

Recall that WEP is a symmetric algorithm that uses the same key for encryption and decryption. Both the sender and the receiver must have the same key for the operation to go well. Plus, if they must share keys, there has to be a way for them to exchange those shared keys securely. The sharing needs to be done this way to prevent intrusion from others.

There is not much detail regarding the management of keys in the 802.11 standards. In fact, key management is the most crucial aspect of a cryptographic system. Apparently, key management is left to the user, according to the 802.11 systems. Key management is one of the reasons why the WLAN environment is suspect to so many vulnerabilities. It also has left key distribution unresolved. What would a layman do to secure the exchanging of keys? Without a proper understanding of how keys should be exchanged securely, one will not be able to use WEP-secured WLANs properly.

When an organization recognizes the need to change passwords frequently and to make them random, it wants to implement changes immediately. However, this kind of task is not easy in a large WLAN environment. There might be 4,000 workstations that need to be changed, and this can get really tiresome. Each of those 4,000 workstations must share the same secret key– and the owner of each workstation must keep the key a secret. Generating, loading, distributing and managing the keys for a large environment like this one poses a serious challenge. If a hacker compromises one client, he or she will have the key to all of the other workstations as well.

Using WPA

Another version of the 802.11 standards is 802.11i. The "i" at the end of the standard indicates a higher version than the previous one. IEEE 802.11i defines the robust security network, which is commonly known as RSN. Any access point that can operate with this standard will allow only RSN-capable devices to connect with it. Consider RSN to be an environment that in evolving with the progress of technology because it provides the security features or services that are required for a network.

However, the IEEE 802.11i standard that is implemented with the use of RSN doesn't mean it is completely perfect. Only time will tell whether there will be flaws in this standard. However, 802.11i features will be mentioned in this section and also when we discuss AES encryptions. Not everyone who likes the idea of hardware and this 802.11i standard will work with the infusion of hardware. Everyone needs improved security, and the use of the hardware in this feature could be a problem. This is where WPA comes to the rescue.

Consider WPA as a solution that improves the solution of WLAN. In laymen's terms, Wi-Fi protected access (WPA) is an initiative that improves WLAN security and most importantly addresses the issues regarding WEP. WPA uses a feature called TKIP (Temporal Key Integrity Protocol), which solves problems without having to fiddle with hardware. In short, WPA modifies the software and firmware drivers to solve problems. Furthermore, TKIP itself is part of the RSN, which allows for flexibility.

WPA is considered a suitable example of a firmware or software patch since it doesn't deal with the hardware directly. As an interim security solution, Wi-Fi protected access does not require a hardware upgrade to the existing 802.11 equipment. However, the IEEE 802.11i standard does require an upgrade. Nothing is perfect, and this is why we can say that WPA is the best when it comes to security features. Regardless, WPA is still a good choice because of the way it attempts to deliver enhanced protection against chronic WEP problems, which predate the availability of 802.11i security features. There are two key features of the WPA:

- 802.1X support.

- TKIP (Temporal Key Integrity Protocol)

WPA uses 802.1X port access control to distribute keys on a section-by-section timeframe. The biggest advantage of this is that it provides a framework that allows for the use of robust upper layer authentication protocols.

Unlike 802.1X, which provides a key distribution-per-section feature, TKIP gives you more. The temporal key integrity protocol allows for key mixing and also gives you a longer IV (initialization vector). However, it doesn't end there. TKIP also provides you with a Message Integrity Check, known as the MIC. You know that when you transmit data over a wireless network, there is a chance that your transmitted data is being tapped into? MIC comes to the rescue because it prevents wireless data from being modified during its transmission. Moreover, these features provide additional support for wireless network security, including:

- Management of keys.

- Extension of the IV space.

- Facilitation. Cryptographic keys should be changed frequently. However, TKIP helps you facilitate the use of session keys.

- Four new algorithms that help you enhance the security of your 802.11.

- Key distribution and derivation.

- Per-packet key construction.

- All of these attributes also mean that it provides cryptographic integrity as a whole.

It is accurate to say that the Temporal Key Integrity Protocol protects against numerous security attacks that were mentioned earlier. Some of the attacks include replay attacks or attacks on data integrity. Most importantly, TKIP helps you change keys frequently, which is a great attribute. The main objective of WPA was initially to bring a standard-based security solution to the marketplace to replace WEP until the IEEE 802.11i RSNs (which were based on an amendment to the existing WLAN standard) became available. It is important to note that RSN includes AES encryption for integrity confidentiality.

WPA itself is nowhere near perfection because it also has its problems. It is possible for a hacker to crack Wi-Fi Protected Access pre-shared keys that consist of short passphrases based on words that could be located inside the dictionary. Dictionary-based keys are easy to crack because the hacker can monitor a short transaction that only takes a few seconds to complete. The hacker can see the speed of typing and the length of the string that was entered.

Other means of security have tools that prevent them from being attacked easily. WPA also has its own software/tool thatcan be used in cracking keys. You can use the tool called "WPA Cracker" (download at **www.tinypeap.com/page8.html**). This tool is somewhat primitive in the sense that it requires you to enter the accurate information retrieved via a sniffer. For learning, it is recommended to use ethereal as your sniffing tool.

While using WPA, you can protect yourself by following these guidelines:

- Make sure you choose a good passphrase. Do not use a passphrase made of words that can be found inside a dictionary.

- Make sure your passphrase consists a minimum of 20 characters. You can avoid a brute force attack with this as well.

- Randomly chose your passphrase.

- Make sure you use WPA Enterprise – or better still, use 802.1X with WPA.

- Make sure you use a VPN (Virtual Private Network) technology.

WPA, RSN and TKIP are very complex topics and there is lots of research still being done in these areas. You can find additional information on the web if needed.

ORGANIZATION ENCRYPTION ATTACK COUNTERMEASURES

Being safe doesn't apply to homes only because organizations are not immune to attacks. This is why an organization should adopt the strategies provided for a home network where practical. Whichever strategy you adopt should be supplemented with either of the measures below:

- WPA2 technology

- VPN technology

USING WPA2

This is an upgrade to the previous WPA, as indicated by the "2" at the end of "WPA2". However, regardless of the upgrade of certain tools, some things will always remain the same. For example, if you are using an old version of "WhatsApp," the new version won't stop sending messages to people on your contact list. WPA2 is still based on a RC4 algorithm, which is a stream cipher. On the other hand, the major component of RSN is the use of AES (Advanced Encryption Standard) encryption for both its data integrity and confidentiality. With the boost of the technology market on a daily basis, you can find products named AES WRAP (Wireless Robust Authenticated Protocol). However, the final specification of this AES WRAP requires the AES-CCMP algorithm, which stands for Counter Mode Cipher Block Chaining MAC Protocol.

As specified in the 802.11i standard, WPA2 helps you enhance message integrity and also protects message privacy. Furthermore, it prevents replays and repudiation.

The 802.11i specification offers you AES-based cryptographic services at the data level. This offering validates them according to the FIPS 140-2 (Federal Standard). This is because the advanced encryption standard is capable of mitigating most of the concerns you may have about active wireless attacks or wireless eavesdropping. If you have a wireless protocol present at the data link level, it will protect only the wireless subnetwork, not the entire network. There are some cases in which high-level protection could be needed. For example, you may have traffic traversing other network segments such as local or wide area networks, the internet and wired segments. There might be a need to consider additional security here. When we talk about additional security, we are talking about implementing higher level, FIPS-validated, end-to-end (E2E) cryptographic protection.

If you use the WhatsApp messenger on your smartphone, you should have noticed the new form of encryption, which is now end to end. This also makes it impossible for the developers of the app to spy on their users' transmitted messages. The AES-based solution provides a highly robust security stance for the future. The only issue with this encryption is that it requires new custom hardware and protocol changes. Many organizations, including yours, could have difficulties implementing the use of AES because it will require you to build a PKI (Public Key Infrastructure). However, this is not a practical solution for many organizations because it is expensive.

There seems to be no cracking tool for AES-CCMP. This is brilliant because we now have security that is totally impenetrable. However, this can be justified only with time because there are many crackers out there who are working to break it down. It is possible that a tool to crack it already exists. Therefore, you need to remain vigilant and stay up on your game.

USING A VPN

Ever seen people in the United States browsing your network as a citizen of the United Kingdom? VPN makes this fun play possible. Your organization can supplement the previously mentioned controls with a VPN (Virtual Private Network). This is a network that is created when public wires are connected to private nodes. You can think of VPN as a secure tunnel that is built within the internet. A VPN's "wall" is made of high-level encryption measures. Moreover, a VPN is attractive because it requires less investment in hardware. In general, whenever you are connected to the internet in a public space, your information can be accessed by others easily. Trying to access your Facebook account while you are sipping juice outside the park is dangerous if you do not use a VPN. This is because the person sitting next to you or even a bit farther away in the park can decrypt or intercept your work with the use of the tools we mentioned in this chapter. In general, you need to install and use VPN technology to protect yourself from malicious hackers whenever you use a public wireless network.

There are three types of VPN:

- **Remote Access VPN:** This is the most common type of VPN. It gained its popularity from the capability it gives a remote user to securely access internal applications (for instance, e-mail).

- **Extranet VPN:** This type of VPN allows one organization to securely access another organization without being detected.

- **Intranet VPN:** In this type of VPN, the data transmitted in the organization's network is encrypted.

There are many platforms available on the internet today that will teach you how to create a network for the purpose of data transmission. Typically, a VPN ensures that only the authorized user can access the network; no other person without authorization will be able to intercept the data. It's like if you wanted to build your house inside the forest without anyone knowing about it and only the person to whom you gave directions would be able to visit you. VPN sets up a kind of tunnel for two networks that only an authorized user can access. When you need the tunnel, you set it up, and when you are finished using it, you close it off. Instead of E2E cryptographic applications, the organization you work with may find it necessary to build tunnels over the public networks at the transport layer. There are different kinds of VPN solutions, ranging from commercial applications to sophisticated features that are available as part of the operating systems we use on our computers. A few of the available **protocols for VPNs** are listed below:

- **PPTP**: **Point-to-Point Tunnelling Protocol**

- **L2TP**: **Layer 2 Tunnelling Protocol**

- **IPSec**: **Internet Protocol Security**

- **SSH**: **Secure Shell**

USING MICROSOFT'S PPTP

This technique is an incredibly quick and relatively easy method of accessing your network. If you are a small business owner, you might also consider using a point-to-point tunneling protocol for your network. PPTP offers a level of encryption that is adequate for most business owners. Most small and medium-sized business owners prefer PPTP because it doesn't require a certificate server and supports native Windows commands. Even most commercial VPN vendors support this protocol. With the point-to-point tunneling protocol, you can choose authentication that uses passwords. However, you need to understand one crucial fact about PPTP: It relies heavily on your skills when it comes to password generation.

USING L2TP

Unlike the point-to-point tunneling protocol, which is available for all Microsoft Operating systems, the layer two tunneling protocol is available only on the Windows 2000 and 2003 platforms. As good as it is, it has a setback. It requires a certificate server or a third-party certificate. However, this can be expensive and not affordable in many cases.

USING IPSEC

This is an industry standard for encryption that Microsoft included in Windows 2000, Windows XP and the 2003 operating systems. This protocol is straightforward to use between Windows machines and also offers excellent security. It also has a setback, just like the L2TP, and requires the use of a certificate server.

There are two modes in IPSEC, which are transport and tunnel. The tunnel mode encrypts the header and also the payload of each packet. However, the transport mode encrypts only the payload.

USING SSH2

This protocol is very useful in organizations. Secure Shell is another tunnel that is mostly used in organizations to tunnel services that have cleartext passwords, such as FTP and Telnet. On the other hand, this protocol gives you flexibility when you try to log into a remote host computer securely. You will also have the ability to run commands on a remote machine and you will enjoy encrypted, secured and authenticated communication between two networks or machines.

However, you should not have the impression that VPN is a completely secure silver bullet. The malicious hackers out there can still mount client-side and server-side attacks on VPNs. Don't forget that your malicious hacker will take time to find your weaknesses. If your weakness is your client, that is where you will be attacked.

CHAPTER SIX: FLAWS IN WEBSITES AND WEB APPLICATIONS

There is perhaps nothing we can do on the web that does not require the use of websites or web applications, particularly with the increase in accessibility of the internet, the proliferation and improvements in web design, and the growth of web application development.

Even though there has been an increase in productivity and ease of use, there is a growing concern about how safe we are on the web, including the security of our information and general presence on the web. There have been many popular cases of security failures, including picture leakages, customer information leaks and more recently the Ransomware virus. There has also been an increase in the desire for the average web user to be more security conscious and to make efforts to guard his or her private data. More plugins and other applications have been developed to guard against spyware and trojans from websites that have downloadable software. Others are designed to warn the users when they are attempting to surf an unsecured website.

However, to effectively protect yourself when using websites or web apps, you must understand the different ways in which your information may be leaked and accessed. There are four levels to note when you are using a website or a web app. These levels are mentioned below, from the base level to the top level.

1. **The database**: This is where the client information is held– where all of the signups are stored, including locations, email addresses and other vital information that the application or website needs to function properly.

2. **The web server:** This is the portal that acts as the interface between the application or website and the files of data. It is

like a door into the warehouse that allows you to retrieve whatever you want so long as it exists. It is a software or computer that provides content to users based on the type of request made from the browser via HTTP.

3. The website or web application: This is the interface we see and interact with when we are surfing a website or using a web app. This holds the codes used in developing and designing the website. It contains the instructions to the server for file retrieval or storage and instructions on how to respond to various user inputs or actions on the website or web app interface.

4. The browser: We all know web browsers are used to display web pages. Some would argue about the importance of this, but I can tell you confidently that it matters as much as the other layers when security and privacy are concerned. Previously, most of the codes were run on the web server. In recent times however, due to the improvement in many client-side scripting languages like JavaScript and various frameworks, more web app codes run on browsers now. These web browsers store lots of pieces of information like cookies, the most frequently visited websites, bookmarks, usernames and passwords.

Now, flaws in the database pose an enormous risk for clients or users of the website or web app. These flaws can allow easy access to the database and expose pieces of information like the client's name, location, account numbers and even social security number. Loose webserver security also reveals information that should otherwise have been protected when sending requests to the server by the website. Information leakage from the application or website itself can occur through errors that were made during programming or development of the website or app. These errors often have to do with user input validation, insecure instructions to the server by the application or website itself, or even comments that reveal the structure of the application or website. For browsers however, the significant amount of information they store (passwords, favorite websites, etc.), makes them a sweet spot for hackers to exploit. If the hacker accesses information like favorite websites, he or she can create a clone website to redirect the user and collect vital information. The hacker can also use flaws that are present in website flash codes or JSON to get information from the user.

The common security flaws that can exist in websites or web apps are mentioned below. It is said that to correctly secure your website or web apps, you need to understand how these security flaws occur and how they can be exploited.

1.   Information leakage

This occurrs when an app or a browser sends information to the server and that information–which should otherwise have been protected or hidden–is shown to the user or hacker. In this context, information has been leaked. This basic security flaw occurs in the coding or application development process. It details how the website or the web app is structured, as well as how information flows in the whole process. If a hacker obtains the relevant codes, he or she can then exploit the website or web app. There are two primary ways in which this information breach can occur:

Directory browsing: Before we explain how directory browsing can leak information, let's explain what it is. On the web, there are two ways of looking for resources, information or content. The first is through search engines, among the most popular of which is Google. Search engines are web applications that use an automated tool or script called spiders or crawlers. These crawlers go through the web, identify keywords, read the contents of the page and follow related links on those pages. They store every single page they visit and every subsequent page on the web server. Thus, when you search a keyword, you get a list of pages that have been stored or indexed on the server. A web directory, on the other hand, is a directory or list of websites that have been classified into various categories. These lists are managed and handled by people. Website owners submit their websites to the directory and the people managing the directory then vet the websites to confirm they meet the criteria for listing in their directory. If we are seeking information for research, want authentic content, or want a broad range of resources related to a particular topic, we will want to use a web directory. When the directory browsing tag in the HTML is indirectly configured, or when files that should be private are listed in the directory, a malicious user can access the file and gain critical information. DirBuster is a tool on Kali Linux that does this task. This application scans a website and its port, which can be 80 or 443 depending on whether it is a secured website. It then uses a wordlist to search for directories in the website that should not be visible. If any of those directories are found, they could lead to the database and cause significant information leaks. To prevent unauthorized access to directories or files by a malicious user, it is advisable to properly configure the .htaccess file or the appcmd command depending on whether you are using the Apache server or the IIS server for your website.

Comments on the HTML page: This is primarily a coding problem that arises when deploying a website or web app. Programming best practices require that a programmer comment a block of code to explain how things function and why the code is structured the way it is. Sometimes developers also mention variables and database names that store information and how this information is used throughout the application process. This is especially important when multiple programmers work on a single project. However, when deploying the website or web app, it is necessary to remove these comments from the codes. When viewing a website on a browser, right-clicking on the page and choosing the view page source option opens a separate window where all of the HTML codes and some JavaScript codes are displayed. These codes were used in the building of the website or web app. On Kali Linux, a plugin named WebScarab can be used to filter out only the comments on a web page. This is done by choosing the fragment and the comment option in the fragment tabs drop-down menu. To prevent this type of information leak, it is necessary to remove the comments that contain sensitive information about the web app. To be extra careful, one can choose to remove all of the comments.

2. Authentication issues

Authentication is a critical aspect of web security. This is when the application verifies the credential or login details of a user and confirms his/her presence in the database of the application or website. This should not be confused with authorization. Authorization is the process of allowing users or clients to access files they have been permitted to access after authentication is completed. Authentication is achieved using the username and login information provided by the user of the website or web app. Below are the common types of authentication protocols employed in websites and web apps.

HTTP-Basic authentication: This is the use of a username and password in authenticating a user. When a user provides his/her username and password for access in an HTTP-Basic authentication-based site, that information is sent in an encrypted format via a base64 encoding system. The username and password are sent in the form of "username: password" before they are encoded using the base 64 algorithm. However, this encrypted information can be intercepted if hackers decide to use tools like Burpsuite and Wireshark. The issues with this authentication system come from the base 64 encoding system, which can be easily decrypted because Wireshark automatically decrypts the encrypted credentials. Also, the usernames and passwords are transmitted in plain text with a colon(:), so they are very susceptible to eavesdropping. Using SSL can limit the risk associated with this type of vulnerability.

HTTP-Digest authentication: This authentication type was developed to combat the security issues of the HTTP-basic authentication. In this type of authentication, the server produces a random value called the 'nonce.' This nonce is used in combination with the username, password, nonce value, HTTP method and URL of the page in creating an encrypted message that is sent to the server. This message is encrypted using an md5 algorithmic encryption that cannot be decrypted backward, as in the case of HTTP-Basic authentication. For decryption to be possible, a hacker must be aware of those four credentials that are used in the encryption process. However, if a malicious user can recreate the same digest message to the server, he or she would be granted access. To restrict these types of attacks, servers often create timestamps with the nonce value so that any time an access request is sent to the server, the server checks the time stamp associated with that nonce value and allows access if the time is not exceeded.

Form-Based authentication: The most common form of authentication used on websites is form-based authentication. Here, the client provides a username and a password on the login page. Login pages are usually created with an HTML <input> tag. When information is entered into the tag, the information is transmitted to the server, where the credential is removed from the input tag, associated with a variable name and then checked against the username and password database. The server then returns a response that verifies the identity of the user or denies the user access to some areas of the website or web app. This type of authentication does not have a predefined way of encrypting the login information it receives, making it very customizable. However, the information is also shared in plain text unless SSL is used. Form-based authentication is very susceptible to brute-force attacks if hackers decide to use tools like Hydra in Kali Linux. Brute forcing is a password-guessing way of gaining access. It requires a username and a password list in which the credentials are cross-applied to the server to get the appropriate login details. For instance, if a username list contains five usernames and a password list contains five possible passwords, the brute forcing tool will try the five possible passwords for each of the usernames, creating a total of 25 login attempts. This list is built during the information-gathering process using social engineering.

3.   Injection-based flaws

Injection flaws are perhaps the most common and devastating flaws that can affect a website or web app. The client basically injects malicious code or script into any input field on a website or web app. This information is sent to the server and if the application is poorly designed, the server executes the commands that were present in the code and allows the client to access sensitive data or the root folder of the app. This always occurs when the application inadequately validates the input data, which allows the hacker to trick the application into performing undesired actions. Ultimately, this causes the hacker to gain control of the application. The two **common types of injection-based flaws** are:

Command injection: This type of injection-based attack targets the operating system of the server itself. The code is written with the input data that is submitted to the server. Applications that send shell commands to the server for information retrieval are very susceptible to command injections. These codes are usually shell commands that can be run by the server. Without a proper input validation system, the server executes the code that was sent to the server, allowing the hacker to access the server. Applications developed with an interpreted language are more prone to injection attacks.

SQL injection: This is by far the most common of the two types of injection attacks listed here. Every website or web app is considered incomplete without a database. This is the lifeblood of the web app itself. A relational database is the most popular form of database associated with websites and web apps. A relational database is essentially the product of storing information in a table that contains rows and columns. Interacting with this database is perhaps the most critical operation that a website or web app performs. To enable the web app or website to interact with this database, requests must be made for information present in that database; in addition, fresh data must be added to the database and existing data must be edited or modified. The application uses SQL commands to achieve this feat. Among programmers, it is called "querying the database." Input forms, cookies, URL properties or variables like headers and XML requests can be used to send malicious instructions to the database, which trick it into divulging sensitive data like usernames, passwords and credit card information. Applications that query the database by binding an SQL command with the user input are also very prone to SQL injection attacks.

The mode of operation is usually to discover the various input fields that exist in an app or website, then to test each field to see how the website responds to each command. This allows us to determine the type of database at play on the website and also to predict whether the website or web app is prone to a SQL injection attack. A command like SELECT, which is used to retrieve information from the database, is by far the most common command sent by the website or web app because a user would almost always need information present in the database. The UPDATE, DELETE and INSERT commands,

106

which are used for modifying, deleting and inputting new information into the database, are also very common SQL commands. During the probing stage of the attack, the hacker tests different commands and observes the response he or she receives. Error reports, in this case, help the hacker identify the operating system and the database type with which the server is working at the time. This also enables the hacker to build a query list that matches the database in question. However, for security reasons, the website may deliver a generic error message without revealing the database type or operating system under attack. This is known as a blind injection attack.

Different tools exist on Kali Linux that make SQL injection possible and easy. One of these tools is Sqlsus. This tool is used to test and exploit MySQL injection flaws. The Sqlninja tool does the same thing, but focuses on the Microsoft SQL server-based database instead. The Sqlninja tool only exploits the flaws; it does not test for them. A more robust tool is the Sqlmap, which supports a large number of databases. It can discover injection flaws, accurately guess the type of database a website or web app uses, and execute commands that give its user total control over the targeted database. This tool is equally effective for both blind injection flaws and flaws that are error based. A tool that focuses on blind injection is the BBQSql, which is a blind SQL injection tool that operates by asking questions and by building the SQL attack based on the responses it gets.

4. Cross-site scripting (XSS) and cross-site request forgery (CSRF)

Cross-site scripting (XSS)

In this age, web apps are being developed to do almost anything online. The uses of these web apps include performing bank transactions, making purchases online, trading in the stock market or bitcoin markets, and even keeping medical records. Due to the increased use of web apps in performing activities of this sensitive nature, it is paramount that they provide protection against hackers who are seeking access to this information. A hacker with access to a user session in a bank app can perform transactions on the person's account or make purchases on the individual's behalf, which is a total nightmare. Therefore, it is essential that a website or web app be secure and that the data provided by any user for any input field be thoroughly checked to ensure it is the legitimate or appropriate data for that particular input field.

Like most of the attacks that occur on web apps or websites, cross-site scripting occurs because of input validation flaws, i.e., when a user input is not properly checked. This allows clients with malicious intent to inject the website or web app with a malicious script and infect users who access that website. Unlike injection-based flaws, cross-site scripting is mostly made up of JavaScript codes that run on the user's browser. JavaScript executes its commands on the browser and not on the web server; this is why cross-site scripting is commonly called a client-side attack. In the early days of JavaScript, creative hackers were able to read data and gain access to data on websites that were open in an alternate or adjacent window. However, with recent improvements in JavaScript and the creativity of hackers, malicious JavaScript codes that are executed on the browser can access the user's cookies and snatch sessions, log the user's key input, scan ports, check the browser's history, find the user's operating system properties and gather other browser data. Cross-site scripting is of three types:

Persistent XSS: In persistent cross-site scripting, a hacker sends a malicious script which is stored in the database or web server of the website or web app. Any time a user visits that website, the malicious code is sent and executed on that user's browser. Because the script exists in the database or the web server, the script is sent to a user's browser without filtering the data. This is why it is also called stored XSS. Popularly targeted platforms for the persistent XSS are social networking platforms, review sections of an e-commerce website or web app, news websites and web forums. The mode of operation usually involves the malicious user testing the various input fields of a website or web app. Then he or she inserts a malicious code in a particular field that does not have an adequate filtering system, which is usually a field that displays the input parameter after it has been sent (for example, the comments section). This code is then sent and stored in the database or the server so that any time another user comes to that particular field, the server deploys that code and executes it on that user's browser.

Reflective XSS: A reflective XSS is a targeted XSS attack. Because the goal of an XSS attack is to execute a malicious script on the user's browser, the hacker first cooks up the script and binds it to a URL. Then he or she sends the link to the user who is being targeted. This link is often sent in the mail, cajoling the victim to click that link. Once that user clicks on the link, the user is directed to the website in the URL and the script is executed automatically, allowing the attacker to use his/her browser for sinister deeds. Contrary to the persistent XSS attack in which the script is saved in the database or web server, in the reflective XSS attack, the user is sent the link where clicking the link executes the script in his or her browser.

DOM (Document Object Module) XSS: In both the persistent and reflective XSS, the user's browser gets a response from the server, assumes it is a legitimate response and then runs it. JavaScript, as we know, is used for displaying dynamic web content and refreshes the web page without fully reloading that web page, like when a website displays live scores. This kind of XSS is done in the browser without getting to the web server at all. Websites that execute JavaScript codes using user input, especially for a GET response kind of site, are very susceptible to this type of attack. It is carried out by inserting a malicious script where an otherwise legitimate script should have been present, making the browser execute that script as if it were the original, legitimate script.

Cross-site request forgery (CSRF)

Cross-site request forgery is not like the XSS attack. In the XSS attack, the hacker takes advantage of the trust the user has placed in that website, making the user accept instructions received via that website. However, in the CSRF attack, the hacker takes advantage of the user's trust in the website or web app. The website or web app believes and executes any command the user gives to it once the user is authenticated on the website or web app. A web app that does not re-authenticate the user on every request is prone to CSRF attack. The attacker cajoles the user to click on a link which runs the code in the browser. That code then allows the attacker to hijack the user's session on the web app or website and performs activities on behalf of that user. For example, a user who has been authenticated on a banking app may be sent a link containing a script that hijacks his/her session and makes the money transfer from his/her account into the hacker's account. This attack is not only limited to fraudulent transfers; it can also be used to make purchases online, change email addresses and vote online.

A good way to mitigate this kind of attack is to use a re-authentication or captcha system to check each request the user makes before execution.

5. File Inclusion Vulnerabilities

File inclusion attacks occur in two separate ways: remote file inclusion and local file inclusion. The file inclusion attack is caused by, as you might have guessed, insufficient or bad user input validation. In this type of attack, a user with malicious intent can execute a command on the server by calling a script on the server (local file inclusion) or a remote server (remote file inclusion). This type of vulnerability occurs mostly on PHP written programs. The PHP syntax uses the "include" keyword in referencing codes that were written separately but that need to be implemented in the present program. For instance, a piece of code may be written to provide navigation for a page; the programmer may need to include this code in each page to enable the user to navigate the website easily. The programmer implements this by using the include functionality present in PHP. This functionality is essential for code reusability, as it eliminates the need to write new codes, thereby saving time in the developmental process.

A remote file inclusion attack can be made when the malicious hacker discovers that the user input causes the app to access a script. When the request is sent in HTTP, the attacker can edit the address to include a script on a remote server. Thus, when that website loads, it executes this script retrieved from that remote server. The local file inclusion attack occurs essentially the same way, except that it accesses a script present on the same web server as the app.

File inclusion attacks can be lethal. They can be used to hijack a user's session; they are capable of stealing cookies and tokens present on the client's browser. They can also be used to steal data or even take control of the total application in the case of a web application.

However, this type of website or web app attack can be appropriately dealt with by taking some vital steps. The website or web app should limit the capacity of a user input that calls a script by using the include functionality. If this cannot be eliminated, the input should be properly validated and restricted in terms of the number of user input characters allowed. The app or website should reject special characters or characters that are not needed. The best way to avoid the file inclusion attack is simply to ensure that user input is properly validated once it is entered.

6. Session-based flaws

A session is the time a user spends interacting with a website or web app. Whenever a user logs onto a site with his or her login details, the server authenticates the user and provides him or her with a session token. Session tokens are very important, as they prevent the user from having to log in every time a request is sent during interaction with the website or web app. This token is often a random long number and serves as automatic re-authentication with the web server. This essentially means that a token was like your login credentials when you were logging onto the website at the beginning of your session, and it should be strictly protected. If an attacker were to gain access to your tokens, he or she could easily impersonate you in the interaction with that web app or website.

Tokens are passed from the server to the browser in the URL of the website or the cookies, or even in hidden form fields. The hacker can steal these tokens using various methods. Some of the more popular methods are:

Man-in-the-middle attack: This is conducted primarily on websites using Secure Socket Layer (SSL) protection. To the user, the hacker pretends to be the server, while to the server, the hacker pretends to be a legitimate user. This allows the hacker to get the information being sent from the user to the server and also the data being sent back from the server to the user.

Packet or data sniffing: This is when the hacker sniffs the data packet sent on a communication channel for information.

This occurs mostly in communications that do not use the Secure Socket Layer (SSL).

Brute force: Some websites create tokens in a particular, definite format or even reuse tokens. If the hacker can get enough tokens to analyze and is using machines with excellent computing abilities, he or she can brute force the tokens and generate legitimate tokens that can be used when accessing the website.

Using an XSS attack to steal tokens: Since we have talked a little about XSS attacks, I believe you have an idea of what happens here. The attacker waits for the user to log into the web app and the server to send the token, which is then saved in the browser. Next, the hacker performs a cross-site script attack and tricks the user into executing it on his or her browser. This executed script is often a token-stealing script that sends the token to a remote server. The hacker can then use this token to interact with the website or web app.

Session fixation attack: This type of attack is very common for sites that send their tokens in the URL. The hacker visits a website or web app, logs in and is given a token. The hacker then crafts a URL with the token he or she has received and sends the link to the targeted user. The user is cajoled into visiting that website with the link and also logs in using that token. However, once the user logs in, he or she is not given a new token because he or she is using an existing token. Once the hacker has confirmed that the user has logged in with that session ID, the hacker does the same and hijacks the session from the user. So, in essence, the hacker gets a token, fixes it on a URL and persuades the user to log in with it.

To protect against session-based attacks, we need to ensure that our website or web app is not vulnerable to cross-site scripting attacks (XSS), as this would make it easy to run token-stealing scripts. You should ensure that tokens and sessions are properly managed. In addition, sending tokens through URLs is highly discouraged. You should also ensure that all user-provided tokens are rejected, as the task of generating tokens should be left to the server.

7. **SSL-Based Vulnerabilities**

Because websites and web apps serve a lot of purposes, security is paramount. Whenever web apps or websites operate, the transmission of data occurs. Information transmitted between the web app and the database might be sensitive information that could be used for sinister purposes if it were to fall into the wrong hands. With the improved creativity and availability of tools capable of sniffing data transmissions and even altering them before they get to the server or client, a need exists for an increase in security when transmitting data. When data packets are intercepted and sessions are hijacked, they could grant access to the database, thereby exposing and compromising the operating system on which the web app or website is based. Using a disk encryption system and tokens can protect data in the database, but not when this data is being transmitted. So, to combat issues related to the security of transmitted data, the SSL or Secure Socket Layer was created.

The Secure Socket Layer encrypts data being transmitted in its period of transmission. If an attacker happens to intercept that data, it would be useless to him because he would have to decrypt the data. The SSL secures the data transmission between the client and the server. The data being transferred through the SSL is encrypted before it is sent to the client or server, which then decrypts the message upon receipt with the help of a decrypted key included in the data transmission. However, the SSL, which was created in 1994, has been replaced by the more secure TLS. The replacement of the SSL was in large part due to its being prone to CRIME, POODLE and BEAST attacks. As you can probably tell, the POODLE is not a dog and the BEAST, in this case, is not an animal.

POODLE, which stands for Padding Oracle On Downgraded Legacy Encryption, is a result of a man-in-the-middle attack (MITM). The hacker initiates a man-in-the-middle attack on the user, takes total control of the router and then forces the browser to downgrade its SSL to a less secure protocol. The hacker then hacks the protocol and steals the information. However, in the BEAST, which stands for Browser Exploit Against SSL and TLS attacks, the hacker tries to guess each character of the encryption key used to protect the information being transmitted.

There are two main methods of encryption involved in using the Secure Socket Layer (SSL) transmission: asymmetric and symmetric.

Asymmetric encryption: In this encryption type, when data is transmitted, it is done with a key (a public key), and once it gets to its destination it is again decrypted by a separate private key. To make this explanation of the concept a little more understandable, let's use this analogy. Assume you have colleagues with whom you share sensitive information. Let's call these people Bob, Paul, Betty and Mike. You build four different mailboxes (one for each of them) and you give each of them a padlock with his or her respective key. However, you also hold a copy of those keys. Then you buy your own four separate padlocks with keys just for you. Once they bring in their email, they lock it with their padlocks and your padlock as well. Whenever you want to take out the mail, you can unlock the mailbox with your key. In SSL, data is encrypted with a public key when it is transmitted and decrypted with a private key when it gets to its intended destination.

The asymmetric encryption model is a secure model. The popular asymmetric encryption algorithm used includes the

Elliptical curve cryptography (this is commonly used in handheld devices), Rivest Shamir Adleman or the RSA (this is the most popular asymmetric algorithmic encryption used today) and the Diffie-Hellman key exchange (this is perhaps the first asymmetric algorithm developed for data transmission).

Symmetric encryption: Unlike in the case of asymmetric encryption, the same key is used for encrypting and decrypting the data. The two major ways by which the symmetric algorithm works is through Block cipher (in this type of symmetric encryption model, the data is encrypted in blocks) and Stream cipher (the transmitted data is encrypted bit by bit).

The algorithms used in symmetric encryption are DES, AES and IDEA, which stands for Data Encryption Standard, Advanced Encryption Standard and International Data Encryption Algorithm, respectively.

In a Secure Socket Layer (SSL) connection, the browser creates a key which is sent to a server, and the server authenticates this key. Then the data to be sent to the server is encrypted using the key previously generated for that session. A hashing function is used in authenticating or testing the integrity of the shared information. In an SSL connection, there is always a separate key exchange algorithm, an authenticating algorithm, a separate encryption algorithm and a unique hashing algorithm. These constitute the information initially shared between the client and the server to ensure proper encryption and decryption in the communication process.

In an MITM – man-in-the-middle – attack, the hacker first attacks the user's computer by posing as a server and using a fake certificate. The user's browser then informs the user that the site's certificate is fake. However, if the user continues creating the connection despite the warning, the user creates an SSL connection with the hacker. The hacker is then able to sniff and intercept the information being sent in the Secure Socket

Layer. The hacker then proceeds to create an SSL connection with the originally intended server posing as the original user. However, since the hacker has been able to intercept the connection with the user, the server assumes the hacker is the user and completes the connection with the hacker.

Tools in Kali Linux give us the ability to create an SSL connection and initiate a man-in-the-middle attack. Some of these tools come with the ability to create a fake certificate for authentication with the targeted user or client. Some widely known and used tools in testing SSL weakness and initiating a MITM attack are:

- SSL split tool
- SSL strip tool
- SSL strip tool
- SSL scan tool
- Open SSL tool

Some of these tools can scan SSL connections and determine the kind of key, authentication, encryption and hashing algorithm combination used in a connection. While the SSL strip tool can generate a certificate and trick the browser into believing it is communicating with the server, the SSL sniff tool fools the user into believing that a server can accept an unsecured connection.

PHISHING

Phishing is a popular web attack used by both scammers and hackers. By pretending to be an authentic and trusted authority, it manipulates the victim into giving out personal information. The hacker can achieve this by pretending to be a representative of an IT company or bank, an employee of an online payment system or even a friend from a social media website. Phishing is a social engineering attack technique. It attempts to pull a user to a website that is often a clone of an original website with which the user is familiar or that the user visits frequently.

Phishing is usually achieved by cloning a legitimate website in the hopes of getting the user's login details. The website is cloned to look exactly like the original website; a piece of code is written that collects the username and password used on the website. That information is then saved in a remote location, usually in text format. Next, this cloned website uses the user's login credentials to create a login attempt on the original site so the user will be logged into the original website. This is a very important step in the phishing procedure, as it is essential that the victim does not suspect foul play during his or her attempt at logging into the website.

The user is also cajoled into visiting the cloned website through the use of a phishing email that prompts the user into clicking a link that redirects the user to the cloned website. The Social Engineering Toolkit in Kali Linux is an important tool in achieving this feat. The social engineering tool contains options for cloning a website exactly as it is on the original website. It also contains a tool for sending the mass email to several target email addresses or to a single target email address.

To execute a phishing attack effectively, you must log into your Kali Linux distro, click the application icon, go to BackTrack and choose the Exploitation Tools option on the right. This will display another set of options containing tools like Web Exploitation tools and Physical Exploitation tools. Our focus will be on clicking the Social Engineering tools. We choose the Social Engineering Toolkit. The Social Engineering Toolkit will open the terminal and show a menu containing different social engineering attack tools. We choose the Web Attack Vector option, then choose the credential harvester attack method on option 3. This option would allow us to clone a website.

The credential harvester option opens up a menu containing three options: (1) the web template option which allows the social engineering tool to import a set of pre-defined web applications we can use in the attack; (2) the site cloner, which helps us clone any site of our choosing; and (3) importing our own customized HTML template. Option two would make the Social Engineering Toolkit ask for the IP address on which to listen and for the website to be cloned. Once these two parameters are provided, the toolkit starts cloning the website. When an unsuspecting victim visits this website, the SET collects the username and password. The website clone is typically used with the spear-phishing option, in which the link to the cloned website is sent in a mass email attack to several targets or to just one target.

KEYLOGGERS

Keyloggers are scripts or devices that allow the hacker to track each keyboard or keypad stroke of the victim and save it in a text or readable format. It is a very useful tool for information gathering. Often, keyloggers are programs or scripts that run in the background on the computer on which they are installed, although physical keyloggers exist as USB multiports or as P2S ports to which the keyboard is connected before being connected to the CPU. This type of physical keylogger contains a memory chip that can be removed and checked for all the information and keyboard strokes it has stored. There are also wireless keyloggers that can sniff, intercept and hijack data sent from a keyboard to its receiver. In addition, there is keylogger software that is installed on the target computer. This type of keylogger software runs in the background without interfering with the victim's activity on his or her personal computer.

Software-based keyloggers must be installed on the victim's computer. This can be done in various ways, which we will discuss shortly. A hacker may be aware of a flaw present in an app the client uses and then exploit this vulnerability to trick the victim into visiting a website that downloads and executes the keylogger. The hacker may send the victim links to download an app or file containing the keylogger. When the victim installs this application, it runs the keylogger installation in the background and starts the keylogger program. A hacker may, on the other hand, place the keylogger in a USB drive with an autorun file. When an individual picks up this drive and inserts it into his/her computer, curious about what is on the drive, the keylogger is automatically executed in the background and starts tracking the user's keystrokes.

Most of these types of keyloggers work remotely and need an internet connection to send the keylogs to the hacker. Other types of keyloggers save the keystrokes locally on the victim's computer and require the hacker to have physical access to the computer to retrieve the log files. Keyloggers are also capable of doing more than tracking keystrokes. They can take screenshots and save information copied on the screen and copied to the clipboard.

Keyloggers are powerful programs. They are easy to build, and most are executed as part of a rootkit. Spyware like keyloggers are very powerful, and require minimal coding and resources to run on the operating system. They can fly under the radar and be undetectable by the system's antivirus application. They typically consist of a dynamic link library and an installer which installs these files and enables them to run in the background. The keylogger can be created using the Metaspoilt option in Kali Linux with the meterpreter. The keyscan_start command is used to start up the keylogger, while the keyscan_dump command requests and receives the log files of the keyboard strokes.

Protection against keyloggers is recommended for any PC user. A good way to do this is by installing antispyware on the computer system. Keyloggers can be very sneaky and can avoid detection by the antivirus software on a PC. The spyware tool would search and pick out keyloggers running in the background. Some antispyware also encrypts the keystroke of the keyboard, causing the keylogger to send a jumbled-up logfile to the remote hacker. This encryption technique is also useful against hardware keyloggers. Although there is no one-size-fits-all approach to protection against keyloggers, it is advisable to regularly scan the system, check background processes for odd processes running in the background and avoid downloading and installing suspicious applications.

DISTRIBUTED DENIAL OF SERVICE OR DDOS

DDoS (Distributed Denial of Service) attacks are incredibly fascinating. Unlike the other kinds of website or web app attacks we have discussed, this attack is not a stealth attack. It is a statement attack. It is meant to create a "you are being hacked" awareness in the website or web app owner's mind. This is the kind of attack most used by the infamous hacker group Anonymous.

The method used in creating a Distributed Denial of Service attack involves flooding a website with more traffic than it can handle. This is done by controlling a large number of users or robots that send server requests to the website simultaneously. In the course of this particular action, the server receives more server requests per second than it can adequately serve in that timeframe. This leads to the web app or website being unavailable to its users. There are two ways of achieving this kind of traffic flooding:

- Coordinating hundreds or thousands of users into sending requests at the same time.

- Using robots or bots which flood the website with bogus traffic.

The DDoS attack is different from the DOS attack in that the DOS attack involves one system trying to flood a website. With DDOS, multiple systems with multiple IPs are used. This makes it very difficult for the website or web app to block a single IP, as it is not sure which traffic is real and which is not. The use of bots has this same effect, as they are being bounced from multiple locations. A perfect analogy is the kitchen sink. When you open the tap, a certain amount of water can pass through the drain at once. If the amount of water poured into the sink exceeds the amount that can flow through the drain, the sink fills until the whole kitchen is flooded.

Another way to describe a DDOS attack is by comparing it to a town accessible by just one bridge. This town would be likened to our server hosting the website while the bridge is the bandwidth that website has for serving traffic. The other city to which the bridge is linked is the attacker or hacker trying to shut down the website. If the bridge can allow passage of about 300 cars at a particular time, and if 900 cars drive out of the city on that road at a particular time, the number of cars on the road would overwhelm the bridge. The result would be a bumper-to-bumper traffic jam on the bridge. This could stall the movement of goods to and from the town, deny legitimate users access to the bridge and cripple the economy, which would lead to the loss of millions in revenue if the situtaion were to continue for a long time.

The DDOS attack becomes even more devastating with the availability of free tools that make it easy to launch this type of attack. Such tools cause server crashes and ultimately take down the service. DDOS attacks are usually done for publicity because they are the "statements" of hackers who are trying to gain a reputation or prestige. The following are some of the free tools used in performing a DDOS attack on a server.

Low Orbit Ion Canon (LOIC): This tool is perhaps the most popular free DOS attacking tool available. This tool is so easy to use, as even newbies have no problem utilizing it. This tool has been used by the infamous Anonymous hacker group. It requires only that the user provide the address of the server and does the rest by itself. It also has the ability to control and coordinate other LOIC systems remotely to perform a DDOS attack on a website. However, this tool does not mask your IP address and can cause you to be traced and arrested if you use it for a malicious purpose.

XOIC: This tool is just like LOIC in its ease of use. However, the creators claim it is more secure than LOIC. It has three attacking modes that can be chosen based on the hacker's intention.

HTTP Unbearable Load King (HULK): This is another popular DDOS attack tool that comes with improved security for the hacker. It has the ability to avoid detection during execution of the attack.

RUDY (R-U-Dead-Yet): I could not possibly talk about DDOS attack tools without mentioning our dear RUDY. It executes an attack using an HTTP POST method. It detects forms present on the website and executes its attack using the form fields.

A myriad of free DDOS attacking tools are present on the web. Some hackers remotely install these tools on computers owned by unsuspecting users and can remotely control them to perform a DDOS attack. These types of computers are called zombie computers. However, some of these free tools are created for testing purposes, although hackers have used them to execute malicious server attacks.

Protecting against a DDOS attack should be a top priority in any organization's web or online objective. The basic approach to doing this involves installing a powerful firewall that detects and blocks fake traffic. Traffic sent to the website can also be redirected to another IP address for analysis, detection and rejection. This approach is called sinkholing. Routing the traffic through cleaning centers to sift the traffic is another way to prevent DDOS attacks. For personal PCs, it is important that the user avoids installing software from unknown, illegitimate sources. Most of these types of applications contain trojans which can allow the hacker to remotely access the PC, thereby using the PC in his/her zombie network to execute a DDoS attack. It is also very important to keep the operating system up to date by installing security fixes or patches and by using a great antivirus program.

Waterhole attacks

Hackers have always sought ingenious ways to launch attacks on users. Sometimes these attacks may be focused on individuals, while other times the focus may be a company or organization. On the other hand, a hacker may just cast a broad net and hope a user falls into it. Waterhole attacks are focused attacks that involve a broad net. The attacker focuses on employees of an organization and sets a trap that is meant for at least one of the targeted employees. The concept of the waterhole attack stems from the animal kingdom, in which a predator waits around a watering hole for prey. The predator hides and whenever the prey comes around for a drink, the predator moves in for the kill.

Basically, the hacker identifies an organization to attack, then observes the employees of that organization and discovers the websites that are visited by most of those employees. An excellent website would be a small to average-sized one whose owner is not particularly security conscious. The hacker scans this website for vulnerabilities; once he identifies these flaws, the hacker injects codes in the website that take advantage of these vulnerabilities. Whenever employees visit this website, they are prompted to download contents or visit another page. Once this malicious code is executed on the victim's device through either the download of malware or drive-by attacks, the hacker gains control of the victim's system and can execute attacks on the organization's network for that system.

DRIVE-BY ATTACKS

Sometimes a system is compromised simply when a user visits a compromised web page. This is done mostly by using drive-by attacks. Today, with users accessing a website through a wide range of devices, like smartphones, tablets and computer systems, websites are designed to be more responsive toward changes in screen size, screen resolution and the operating system.

Websites now contain instructions that seek and find details like browser type, Flash and Java plugin versions, and other details necessary for adjusting the website to the client's device. When hackers compromise a web page that contains instructions about this information, they become adequately equipped to launch targeted attacks that are focused on exploiting vulnerabilities in the system's browser or plugins.

Attacks like these are very difficult to detect, so it is important that users ensure their applications and operating systems are always up to date. It is also important to download all security patches as soon as they become available.

CLICKJACKING

This is a user interface redressing attack. The hacker fools the user into clicking on a malicious link when the user intends to click on a legitimate link presented on a website. This type of attack usually flies under the radar and is not as popular as the other website attacks. This particular attack takes your attention from what matters, and before you know it, you have been hacked. In fact, it is a very clever way of hacking.

The attacker visits a website, which is usually a financial or e-commerce site. The attacker navigates to a page that is suitable. The attacker then creates an iframe on that website describing a marvelous offer for money or luxury goods–something the victims would be likely to click. Then he places that frame over the legitimate link on the website that may not interest you but that will serve the purpose of hacking when clicked. You are fascinated by the message and click on the link, which causes money or goods to be sent to the hacker's account or address.

CHAPTER SEVEN: ATTACKING WITH FRAMEWORKS

SOCIAL ENGINEERING

Due to the increase in the use of technology for almost all of our activities, companies and organizations have invested a huge amount of money in ensuring that the technologies they use are properly secured from hackers. These companies have developed and implemented extensive firewalls to protect against any possible security breach. Most internet users are not security conscious despite the ease with which information can be obtained over an internet connection. This is coupled with the fact that most malicious hackers concentrate their efforts on computer servers and client application flaws. Over the years, these hackers have become more creative in how they gather information and structure their attacks on websites and web apps. With the enormous amount of money invested in online security, we would expect that malicious information theft or control would have been eliminated. However, this has not happened.

This is where we use social engineering to achieve our goal. It is a non-technical approach circumvents a company's security measures. No matter how secure a company's online applications are, they are still susceptible to hacking. Hackers have been able to achieve this using social engineering and tools based on social engineering. Social engineering is a hands-on approach to hacking. It involves targeting individuals and manipulating them into giving out vital information that can lead to a breach in the security system. These individuals, who may be employees of the organization or even a close relative of the top person at the target organization, are approached and coerced into trusting the hacker. They begin to gather information that could be of use in the hacking process. This is usually an approach taken when the company's firewalls are effective at thwarting outside penetration. When the hackers have obtained the necessary information (for instance, the login information of the social engineering target), they can hack the company from the inside out.

It is believed that human beings are the weakest link in any information security chain. The physical approach toward social engineering can occur in so many ways that it is impossible to cover all of them in this chapter. However, popular means include approaching and becoming friends with (or even a significant other of) employees at the company. Sometimes the employees are given a flash drive containing movies or other files in which they may be interested. The employees plug in the drive and launch a file that executes scripts in the background, granting the hackers access to the respective machines. The social engineer attack can also occurr when a person calls an employee of a firm, impersonates a call center representative and tells the employee that he or she needs information to rectify a service that is important. The hacker would have gathered details about the employee from the employee's social media account or through personal conversations with the person. Once the hacker has received the information (which may include the victim's social security number or login details), the hacker hijacks the account and performs fraudulent transactions on it, or uses it for additional attacks. Social engineering makes it easy to build a username and password list that helps with logging into the target's accounts.

Hackers use the information they have gathered in combination with tools that ensure an easy hack of the company's system. Most of these tools are used in the client-side attack and are enhanced with the information gathered through social engineering. This information is used in conjunction with phishing and spoofing tools to attack a client if a direct social engineering attack fails. Social engineering is the information gathering procedure in this approach when it comes to attacking clients. Hacking has become a business venture. Hackers gain access to information simply to sell it for money, or to use it to transfer money. The motivation now is monetary. Usually, the target is selected, and the hacker uses information available to the public about the client to develop the attack. Typically, information obtained online is sufficient to build an attack. However, with an increase in employee education regarding hackers and social engineering, employees have begun to limit the personal information they share on social media and other public platforms.

The success of a social-engineering-based attack depends solely on the quality of information gathered. The attacker must be sociable and persuasive when interacting with the victim, such that the victim becomes open and begins to trust the hacker. Some hackers outsource this aspect to an individual who is skilled in getting people to tell them secrets.

Social Engineering Toolkit (SET)

The Social Engineering Toolkit is a very important tool used in a computer-aided social engineering attack. It comes pre-installed with the Kali Linux distro. It is written in the Python language and is also an open source toolkit. The Social Engineering Toolkit, or SET, was created by David Kennedy to exploit the human aspect of web security. However, it is important to make sure that the Social Engineering Toolkit is up to date. Once the tool has been updated, the configuration file can be set. The default configuration file is sufficient to make the SET run without any problems. Advanced users may want to edit and tweak certain settings. However, if you are a beginner, it is better to leave it the way it is until you become more familiar with the Social Engineering Toolkit. To access the configuration file, open the terminal and then change the directory to the SET. Open the config folder and you will find the set_config file, which you can open and edit with a text editor to change the parameters.

The Social Engineering Toolkit can be accessed by clicking on the Application icon, then clicking on the Kali Linux desktop. Next, click on BackTrack and then on the Exploitation Tools option. Click on Social Engineering Tools and select the Social Engineering Toolkit by clicking on SET. The SET will open in a terminal window. Alternatively, the SET can be opened directly from the terminal by typing "setoolkit" without the quotes.

The Social Engineering Toolkit opens in the terminal as a menu-based option. The menu contains different options based on the type of social engineering attack you need to use. The option at number 1 is for spear-phishing vectors which enable the user to execute a phishing attack. The phishing attack is an email attack. It is like casting a net by sending emails to random potential victims. Spear-phishing, on the other hand, targets one individual and the email is more personalized.

The second option on the SET menu is the website attack vector, which uses different web-attack methods against its target victim. The website attack vector option is by far the most popular and perhaps most used option in the Social Engineering Toolkit. Clicking on the website attack vector option opens menus containing the Java applet attack vector, the Metasploit browser exploits, the credential harvester attack used in cloning websites, the tabnabbing attack, the man-in-the-middle attack, the web jacking attack and the multi-attack web method.

The third option on the Social Engineering Toolkit menu is the infectious media generator tool. This is a very easy tool to use and is targeted at individuals who can give a hacker access to the organization network, thus enabling the hacker to hack from inside the network. This tool allows the hacker to create a

USB disk or DVD containing a malicious script that gives the hacker access to the target shell. Choosing this option opens a menu with a prompt to choose from between a file-format exploit or a standard Metasploit executable. Choosing the file-format option opens a list of payloads from which to select. The default is a PDF file embedded in an executable script. This is then sent to the drive where the autorun.inf is created with the PDF file. When an employee opens the file on the drive, the file is executed in the background and the hacker gains shell access to the victim's computer.

The fourth option is the generate-a-payload-with-listener option. This option allows the hacker to create a malicious script as a payload and therefore generate a listener. This script is a .exe file. The key is getting the intended victim to click and download this script. Once the victim downloads the .exe file and executes it, the listener alerts the hacker, who can access the victim's shell.

The fifth option in the Social Engineering Toolkit is the mass mailer option. Clicking this option brings up a menu with two options: single email address attack and the mass mailer email attack. The single email address attack allows the user to send an email to a single email address while the mass mailer email attack allows the user to send an email to multiple email addresses. Choosing this option prompts the user to select a list containing multiple email addresses to which the email is then sent.

Sixth on the list is the Arduino-based attack. With this option, you are given the means to compromise Arduino-based devices. The seventh option, on the other hand, is the SMS spoofing option, which enables the hacker to send SMS to a person. This SMS spoofing option opens a menu with an option to perform an SMS spoofing form of attack or create a social-engineering template. Selecting the first option will send to a single number or a mass SMS attack. Selecting just a single number prompts the user to enter the recipient's phone number. Then you are asked to either use a predefined template or craft your own message. Typing 1 chooses the first option while typing 2 chooses the second option depending on your preference for the SMS. Then you enter the source number, which is the number you want the recipient to see as the sender of the SMS. Next, you type the message you want the recipient to see. You can embed links to a phishing site or to a page that will cause the user to download a malicious .exe file. After the message has been crafted, the options for services used in SMS spoofing appear on the screen. Some are paid options and others are free.

Option eight in the SET is the wireless AP attack vector. This option is used to create a fake wireless AP to which unsuspecting users of public Wi-Fi can connect and the hacker can sniff their traffic. This option uses other applications in achieving this goal. AirBase-NG, AirMon-NG, DNSSpoof and dhcpd3 are the required applications that work hand in hand with the wireless AP attack vector.

Option nine in the menu is the QR code attack vector. Today, QR codes are used everywhere, from the identification of items to obtaining more details about products on sale. Now QR codes are even used to make payments. Some websites use QR codes for logins or as web apps. This login method is used because it is perceived as a more secure way of gaining access due to hackers' being able to steal cookies, execute a man-in-the-middle attack and even use a brute-force password to gain unauthorized access. However, this increase in the use of QR codes has given hackers more avenues for exploiting their victims. The QR code attack vector helps the hacker create a malicious QR code. Then the hacker creates or clones a website like Facebook using the credential harvester option and embeds this malicious QR code with the link to the cloned website. The hacker then sends a phishing email or spoofed SMS to a victim, which prompts that person to scan the code with a mobile device. This reveal's the victim's GPS location and other information when the victim visits the website and enters their login details.

The tenth option in the menu is the PowerShell attack vector. This option allows the hacker to deploy payloads in the PowerShell of an operating system. The PowerShell is a more powerful option than the command prompt in the Windows operating system. It allows access to different areas of the operating system. It was developed by Microsoft to ease the automation of tasks and configuration of files and has come with the Windows operating system since the release of Windows Vista. The PowerShell attack vector enables the attacker to create a script that is then executed in the victim's PowerShell. The selection of this option brings out four menu options: PowerShell alphanumeric injector, PowerShell SAM database, PowerShell reverse and PowerShell bind shells. Any of these options creates a targeted PowerShell program and is exported to the PowerShell folder. Tricking the target to access, download and execute this program creates access for the attacker.

By now, you should realize how powerful the SET is in executing computer-aided social engineering attacks. This tool is very valuable for a penetration tester, as it provides a robust and diverse means of checking the various vulnerabilities that may exist in an organization's network.

BeEF

BeEF stands for Browser Exploitation Framework. This tool comes with most of the security-based Linux distro, like the Parrot OS and Kali Linux. BeEF started as a server that was accessed through the attacker's browser. It was created to target vulnerabilities in web browsers that would give access to the target systems for executing commands. BeEF was written in the Ruby language on the Rails platform by a team headed by Wade Alcorn. As stated before, passwords, cookies, login credentials and browsing history are all typically stored on the browser, so a BeEF attack on a client can be very nasty.

On Kali Linux, however, BeEF has been included in the distro. The BeEF framework can be started by going into applications, clicking on exploitation tools and then clicking on the BeEF XSS framework. This brings up a terminal that shows the BeEF framework server has been started. Once the server has been started, we open our browser of choice and visit the localhost at port 3000. This is written in the URL space of the browser as localhost:3000/ui/authentication   or 127.0.0.1:3000/ui/authentication. This would bring us to the authentication page of the BeEF framework, requiring a login username and password. By default, the username is beef ; the password is also beef.

Once you are in the BeEF framework, it will open a "Get Started" tab. Here you are introduced to the framework and learn how to use it. Of particular importance is hooking a browser. Hooking a browser involves clicking a JavaScript payload that gives the BeEF framework access to the client's browser. There are various ways by which we can deploy this payload, but the simplest way is to create a page with the payload, prompt the target to visit that page and execute the JavaScript payload. You can be very creative about this aspect. On the other hand, there is a link on the Get Started page that redirects you to The Butcher page. Below this page are buttons containing the JavaScript payload. Clicking on this button will execute the script and, in turn, hook your browser. When your browser is hooked, you will see a hook icon beside your browser icon on the left side of the BeEF control panel with the title

"Hooked browser" along with folders for online and offline browsers.

Once a browser is hooked, whether it's online or offline, we can control it from our BeEF control panel. Clicking on the details menu in the control panel will provide information like the victim's browser version and the plugins that are installed. The window size of the browser also can be used to determine the victim's screen size, the browser platform (which is also the operating system on the PC), and a lot more information. For executing commands on the browser, we click on the command menu in the control panel. This brings up a different command we can execute on the victim's browser. This command would create a pop-up message on the victim's browser, so it can be renamed creatively before execution to avoid raising any suspicion. Some of the commands that can be executed in this menu include the Get all Cookie command (which starts harvesting the victim's browser cookies), the Screenshot command, the Webcam command for taking pictures of the victim, the Get visited URL command and so on. There are a lot of commands in this menu.

The BeEF framework JavaScript payload can also hook mobile phone browsers. Checking the details tab after hooking will give that particular information if we end up hooking a phone browser. Clicking on the module and searching the PhoneGap command allows us to execute phone targeted commands like geolocating the device and starting an audio recording on the victim's device. Clicking on the Ipec menu also displays a terminal we can use to send shell commands to the victim's system.

Once the BeEF framework hooks a browser, the possibilities are endless. We can do virtually anything. Therefore, it is important to be careful when clicking links and pop-up or flash messages.

METASPLOIT

The Metasploit framework is perhaps the larget, most complete penetration testing and security auditing tool today. This tool is an open source tool that is regularly updated with new modules for monitoring even the most recent vulnerabilities. Metasploit comes with the Kali Linux distro. It is written in Ruby, although when it was created it was written in Perl. This tool was developed by HD Moore in 2003 and was then sold to an IT company called Rapid7 in 2009.

Metasploit is an immensely powerful tool that has great versatility. To fully utilize Metasploit, you must be comfortable using the terminal, which is a console type window. However, there is an option that allows for the use of Metasploit in a GUI window. Armitage, an opensource tool, makes this possible, although it does not have the capacity to fully utilize all aspects of the Metasploit framework in an attack. The meterpreter in the Metasploit framework is a module that is dumped in the victim's system, making it easy for the hacker to control that PC and maintain access for future hacks in that system. Getting started with Metasploit on Kali Linux is as good as opening the terminal and typing "msfconsole" without the quotes.

Metasploit contains modules that can be used during a hack. Some of these modules are written by developers or contributors from the open source community. An important set of modules includes the payloads. The payloads are very important when it comes to performing attacks within the Metasploit framework. These payloads are codes that have been written so that the hacker can gain a foothold in the victim's computer. Perhaps the most popular among these payloads is the meterpreter. This particular payload is very powerful, as it leaves no trace of a hack on the system's drive. It exists solely on the victim's system memory.

Then there is the Exploits module. These exploits are codes that have been written and packed for specific flaws in a victim's operating system. Different exploits exist for different operating system flaws, so flaws that are targeted for one vulnerability would fail when used for another.

The encoders are modules that encode the different payloads deployed into the target system to avoid detection by the victim's antivirus, anti-spyware or other security tools.

Other modules available on the Metasploit framework are the Post modules (which allow the hacker to gather passwords, tokens and hashes), the Nops modules (most of which allow for 100 percent execution of the payload or exploit) and the Auxiliary modules (which do not fit into other categories).

This framework is quite robust, as many kinds of hacking procedures can be carried out. Several procedures are executed by combining the modules and making them work in different ways. A good way for a beginner to learn more about the Metasploit framework is to type "help" without the quotes in the Metasploit framework console.

CHAPTER EIGHT: PENETRATION TESTING AS A PROACTIVE SECURITY MEASURE AND WEB SECURITY MEASURES

PENETRATION TESTING

Penetration testing is ethical hacking. For every asset we own, we must provide adequate security, even more so if those assets are being used by other people, who may be our customers. If you run a website that saves or receives sensitive information from your users, your website or web apps must be accessed.

Pentesting: This is another way of saying penetration testing. It is the practice of testing a computer system or web application to find vulnerabilities that an attacker could exploit. It is a certified pretend attack that looks for vulnerabilities and gradually gains access to the system's data. It helps determine security policy compliance, employees' security awareness and an organization's ability to identify and respond to security incidents. It is very effective because it finds some of the most complex attack vectors across systems if an intrusion is made. It can also help detect the attack approach of a hacker and therefore prevent its reoccurrence. Pentesting requires manual and automated testings that are performed by using a vast array of tools.

The process of penetration testing may be simplified into two parts. The first has to do with discovering vulnerabilities including all of the legal processes that allow those testing the network to run illegal operations. The second involves taking advantage of the vulnerabilities to allow access to just one machine, which is meant to exploit a vulnerability. This singular successful exploit opens the door to controlling the other systems in the network. This particular process is known as pivoting. There are many other pentesting strategies, which can be selected depending on the threat they are meant to deal with.

In general, targeted testing is executed by the organization's IT group. This group works together with the penctration group to achieve desired results. Furthermore, external penetration testing is aimed at a company's externally detectible servers or devices, including DNS, web servers and e-mail servers. The primary goal is to determine whether it is possible for a hacker to gain control of the network and if so, how much destruction can be caused.

Blind testing refers to a scenario in which the tester only has the details of the enterprise, like the name of the target. This approach gives security staff some time to investigate the nature of an application attack and where it is most likely to take place.

Penetration testing includes all activities that are undertaken by IT professionals to discover the flaws in a system. Although it is important to stay ahead of new vulnerabilities, it is difficult to stay on top of recent hacking techniques and zero-day malware. This is why it is important to obtain a list of priority tests when doing a security audit.

SECURING YOUR WEBSITE

Providing your website with adequate protection from a hacker is more important than ever before. The website owner must give visitors a safe surfing environment. Adequately securing the website protects it from being infected with malware, protects your visitor's details, improves your web ranking and ensures you continue doing business for a long time. Keep in mind that once your website is hacked, it is very difficult to put it back together. You will lose customers when your website goes down and your reputation will also be lost.

We have talked about the various flaws that can be exploited on the server and client sides of a website. Some of these attacks are very difficult to detect and that is why prevention is the best policy.

If you run a website based on a content management system like WordPress or Joomla, always install security plugins that are available on that CMS. Sitelock is a valuable tool that scans a website daily for flaws, malware and viruses. Investing in a good cloud protection service is also a great idea, as it will filter all of the content that reaches the site and screen out suspicious traffic and bots.

One of the most popular and commonly executed website attacks is the SQL injection. Exploiting this flaw gives a hacker access to private information. This type of attack is executed on websites that have form fields which accept user input. A very good way to prevent this attack is to use parameterized queries. This ensures the website contains parameters that make it impossible to insert malicious codes.

We also talked about cross-site scripting attacks, or XSS attacks for short. We now know that cross-script attacks are a result of JavaScript codes that are executed in the client's browser. As with the SQL injection attack, preventing the XSS attack requires that the programmer or developer state explicitly what entries are allowed in a browser's various user input fields. A great way to do this is by implementing a content security policy, or CSP for short. This will give directions to the browser for different entry fields, including which field should allow for executable scripts and which should not.

For websites that require user login information, it is important to insist on strong passwords when the user registers. Users should create a password that is a mixture of letters, numbers and special characters or symbols. It is also important to ensure that passwords are encrypted when users log into the website.

This measure makes it difficult for hackers to crack the password if they happen to execute a man-in-the-middle attack. Also keep in mind that it takes just one weak password for a hacker to gain access to all of the accounts.

Also ensure that user inputs are properly validated when they are typed in and when they are sent over to the server. This client side and server-side validation ensures that malicious codes are not mistakenly executed. Regarding the browser, on the web page, it is important to define the fields that require input and to also make sure they follow the input field specification. A field that is meant for numbers should reject a letter or a special character input before the content is sent to the server for another phase of input validation.

If you run an e-commerce store, a banking app or any other website that accepts and stores very sensitive information, get an SSL certificate. This provides an extra layer of security for your website. Customers and clients who visit your site will rest easy when they see that "HTTPS" precedes your website URL. This HTTPS encrypts all the information traveling to and from your server. It renders any information being sought by a hacker as useless even if he or she is performing the sniffing attack.

Error messages displayed to the user should be kept minimal. If an error message is to be shown to the user at all, it should not include vital information like the database type or error code. It is a good idea to configure the error message to display a generic message because error messages give a hacker information about the underlying structure of the website or web app, which can be used to coordinate a targeted attack.

It is also important that your admin username and password are very strong. Make sure there is a limited number of login trials on the login page. Ensure that security questions are asked when a user uses the "forgot password" link. Even if the user gets the question right, avoid sending the login username, password or other credentials to the user's email.

Make sure you set strict permissions that need to be granted before anyone can access your files. Ensure that only the admin can edit some files, while keeping other files readable for the website's users. It is also a useful practice to limit the number of files that can be uploaded on your website. Through file uploads, it is easy to embed malicious codes that can open up a website to attacks. Make sure that all uploaded files are saved in a private folder and can only be shown by executing a script written solely for that purpose. Furthermore, you should not allow the uploaded files to reach the root folder.

As with web apps and websites, it is important that we ensure that when coding or working with programmers on a project, we adopt what is known as secure coding practice. Examples of secure coding practice include designing a system for maximum protection against hacks, building each module separately, testing modules for flaws and merging everything together so that the entire application can be tested for other vulnerabilities.

It is also a good policy to keep designs as simple as possible. Complex websites or web app designs are more prone to errors and issues that a malicious user can take advantage of. As mentioned throughout this book, data sanitization is very important for securing your website or web app. Always sanitize the data that is flowing through your application, whether it is coming from the user, the server or even a third-party-linked application.

CONCLUSION

Securing your website, web app and devices is a never-ending process. To get started, you should list all of the devices, networks, websites and web apps you work with. After doing this, analyze each of them and find out the various flaws that can be exploited by a hacker. If you have been attacked before, how did it happen? What were the initial signs before you were hacked? Are those flaws still present in the system or network? What steps did you take to minimize the damage and what steps have you taken to ensure it does not occur in the future? Answering these questions will give you perspective. These questions will help you find parts of your system that could be the focus of an attack and also help you focus more of your security efforts in the right places. They will also help you determine the kind of people you will need for each job and the kind of tools that will do those jobs effectively. You will be able to hire people who have the necessary skills to get the job done without compromising security or quality.

The security tools you use are paramount, as is the implementation of these tools. The security market today offers lots of tools that can take care of a company's security needs. However, just because a tool is more expensive or has a high rating does not mean it is the best tool for you or your team. Price is not a measure of quality and lots of open source tools can provide great solutions for your security needs. The questions you should ask are as follows. What kind of environment are you working in? Does this particular tool work perfectly in that environment? Does your team have the technical know-how to implement this tool? Does it fit seamlessly into your existing network or working tools? Does the cost of using it translate to a significant return on investment? These are important points to consider when selecting a security tool to protect against a vulnerability.

Generally, it is important to always know where your weaknesses and strengths lie. When developing your security policy and planning your security measures, assume the role of the hacker. As a popular saying goes, "Attack is the best form of defense." Analyze your system with the mind of a hacker and assume a hacker's role. How would you compromise your system? Given your own intimate knowledge, how can it be compromised remotely? How can a hacker take control of your system or network from the inside?

Take penetration testing, risk analysis and vulnerability assessment seriously and ensure they are frequently performed on your system. You are as weak as the weakest link in your chain. Train and test your team members so that they can respond to a network or system security breach effectively. If possible, hire a security agency to simulate an attack on your systems and see how they respond. Also, it is a good idea to automate most of your work because automation will ease the implementation of appropriate security measures in your system and make threats easy to deal with when they emerge.

On a final note, always back up your data. Update your data with new changes and ensure the process is properly finished to avoid corrupted backup data that is of no use. This way, you can rest easy without having to worry about data loss.

CHAPTER NINE: LINUX

Linux was developed in the middle of the last century and is an operative system employed by business agencies, industries and computer users worldwide. It exists on almost all available computers, smartphones and similar electronic devices. Linux is the bedrock of the internet and the background of the computing world. It is the brain behind scientific development, computing advancement and technological achievements. Linux is still one of the best operating system ever invented because it is reliable, user friendly and very secure.

WHAT IS LINUX?

Linux is an operating system (OS) that can run on any computer. Operating systems are very strong programs that run in the computer's background and are necessary for other programs to function on the computer. Examples of operating systems include Windows, Mac, Chrome, FreeBSD, etc. An operating system is the bridge between a computer's hardware and software. Without an operating system, the computer is only an engine.

Below are the parts of an operating system.

Bootloader: Before a computer can be used, it must boot through a process that can take a few minutes. This period of booting starts when you switch on the computer. The bootloader is the part of the operating system that oversees this process.

Kernel: This is the lowest level of an operating system, but at the same time the most important. It controls other parts of the operating system as well as activities related to the processing of the system.

Daemons: These are programs on the operating system that run outside the control of the user and act in accordance with the hardware's activities. These activities occur at the interface of the computer or when the computer is running.

Shell: During the era of "old" Linux, people sometimes assumed they had to learn a series of command structures to initiate Linux. With the invention of the new desktop Linux, there is no need for that now. The shell makes it easy for a user to control or use the computer through commands.

Graphical Server: The graphical server or the X server in responsible for displaying images on the monitor.

Desktop Environment: The desktop environment houses various compartments that display different utilities and require reciprocal action from users. It also includes applications and tasks that are carried out on the computer.

Applications: Includes thousands of software that a user can install and run on the computer with the help of the desktop environment. Some desktop environments don't order applications in a regular pattern. Unlike these desktop environments, Linux provides countless types of software that a user might need and install. The Linux desktop environment includes stores that offer a wide range of applications for installation.

WHY IS LINUX IMPORTANT?

Users are curious about the differences between Linux and other operating systems. Why is Linux regarded as one of the best types of software ever invented? In comparison to other operating systems, Linux is very easy to work with and creates fewer problems for users. It is secure against different kinds of hardware problems, including viruses and worms, crashes, licensing fees, monthly upgrades, cleaning and other problems that are associated with other operating systems. It is free because there are no costs related to licensing for a software or server. When we compare the price of a random Linux server with the price of a Windows server, the Windows server could cost about $1,200, excluding the licensing fees of other software you might want to run on it. Also, installing a web database server and other activities is easy because of the server installation guide.

If you are into installation management or maintenance of a computer network, Linux is a good choice. If you still have doubts concerning Linux, consider the fact that users rarely complain about issues related to viruses or unnecessary rebooting. Users can attest to the fact that Linux's servers can run for a very long period of time without restarting.

Linux is also distributed under an open source license. Because of this, it has the following features:

1. Liberty to run the program for any reason.
2. Liberty to understand the program's working principle and to change it in any way that is needed.
3. Liberty to reproduce copies for other purposes.
4. Liberty to share copies with other computer users.

The intent behind the invention of this operating system is clear. It is meant to be a bond servant for any computer user, which means it is meant to relieve users of the burden of using other operating systems. They can assert less effort and reap more effective results. This is why a number of computer users have decided to go with Linux.

DISTRIBUTION

Distribution or "distros" are various forms of Linux that are available to any user. Regardless of your level of knowledge in computing, there is always a Linux version that you can easily work with. These distros are available for free, and they can be transferred using a USB to another computer for various purposes.

Some common Linux versions are:

- Linux Mint

- Red Hat

- Fedora

- Debian/GNU Linux

- Ubuntu

- Centos

- openSUSE

- Protean OS

- Mandriva Linux

- Arch Linux

Each distribution has its own approach and interconnections, some of which are very recent. Ubuntu and Debian are classic examples, while others are attached to old customs. A prime example of this is openSUSE. If you are an average computer user, the only prerequisite for learning Linux is access to a computer that can allow you to install a Linux program. However, some knowledge of programming could be important in other cases. You can begin using Linux for easy tasks like browsing, altering pictures, sending e-mails and listening to audio. The source code of Linux comes in an easy programming language and is available to the public so others can reproduce the software in their native languages.

For beginners, the following versions will be great:

- Ubuntu

- Linux Mint Cinnamon

- Manjaro Linux

- Linux Server

Linux servers are powerful and dynamic versions of the open source Linux operating system (e.g. the Ubuntu server). While you can get some of these servers for free (Ubuntu and Centros), others come with a price tag and are somewhat affordable with additional advantages (SUSE and Red Hat enterprise Linux).

To determine the distribution that would be easy for you to work with, you must consider certain factors mentioned below.

1. Your competence in using the computer.

2. What you would prefer between a server and desktop.

3. Whether you would prefer a modern or traditional desktop interface.

An average computer user would do better to opt for the beginner's distribution, which is very easy to learn and use. Some examples are Ubuntu and Manjaro Linux. However, if you're quite good at handling a computer, you could opt for more difficult distributions like Fedora and Debian. If you're a computer guru, you can upgrade to complex distros like Gentoo.

If your choice is the server type, you'll need to decide between a server distribution and a desktop interface. You will also need to determine whether you will be operating solely by using command lines. It is important to note that the Ubuntu server does not permit the installation of a GUI interface, which means you will need some knowledge regarding the initiation of command lines. Otherwise, your server will be stuck and unable to progress when loading graphics. Another option is to install a GUI package on an Ubuntu server that uses single command lines.

Systems analysts will consider the features of a distribution before making a choice. Which server will best suit your needs? For example, if you need a self-sufficient distribution that will provide all of the necessary requirements for your choice of server, you should choose Centos.

HOW TO SUCCESSFULLY PERFORM A LINUX INSTALLATION

The fact that Linux is a user-friendly operating system cannot be stressed enough. Basically, you just need to follow a few steps. Linux installation can be done directly from a CD or a drive without any alterations to your hard drive. At the beginning of the installation process, simply click on the installation icon displayed on the screen. The installation often comes with an installation wizard that serves as a guide to successful installation of the Linux operating system. The following steps will lead to the successful installation of Linux's Red Hat version. Note that you must ensure your computer is compatible with the Linux version you wish to install. You might also need to include some plugins or third-party software that will be of more use to the program.

1. First, place the Red Hat Linux disc into the hard drive and wait until "install Red Hat Linux" or something similar shows up on the screen. Once that happens, click on "install" and then installation will begin automatically. The program will ask you to confirm whether the disc from which you are installing is

properly inserted. Do not worry about this and just continue with the installation process.

2. Next, you will need to select your preferred language option. A list of several languages to choose from will be provided. After this has been done, you can move on to the next stage of the installation process.

3. The program will then ask for the keyboard that matches your computer. Again, a variety of options will be displayed, from among which you should select the right keyboard type. Once this is done, you can skip to the next part of the installation.

4. Here, the program will ask for the installation code to verify whether you are licensed to use the software. In other cases, you could simply skip this part and move on to the next stage; however, if you wish to fully maximize the program, you will need a licensing code. Once you have correctly entered the code, verification will take place automatically and you will be free to move on to the next step.

5. The next step is to create the installation path or location of the program in your computer's hard disc. Use the available space on the drive and create a layout. Set it as default so as not to interfere with any other operating system on your computer. Create the necessary partitions and their respective sizes for proper functioning of the software.

6. Next, select the network setting. Provide the necessary data for the required network address. Set the proper time. Select your time zone and create the super user password.

7. The final step is to complete the installation process and restart the computer.

Installing any desired app on Linux

Almost every operating system comes with a store containing hundreds of different software programs you can install and uninstall to fully maximize the operating system. The installation process is quite easy, especially when it comes to Linux. Some distributions employ an Advanced Packaging Tool (APT) for easy installation of software. The APT skims the database in the hard drive while searching for programs and their various locations in the drive. Using APT, you can type the name of any software, search for it and install it.

Early versions of Linux were more difficult to handle due to an absence of software tools. Installation was achieved by a complex form of arrangement under a Minix. Installation now commences after the arranged software is transferred to the right locations. With recent advances in Linux versions, distribution comes along with varying software tools, including Portage. Portage is a software tool that is used by the complex Gentoo distribution. The most important thing about these tools is that they have the same primary function of compiling software from various locations for installation. The GUI is a factor that greatly affects these software tools, as many of them need a GUI to function.

For servers that don't employ GUIs, the command line will be the next option. A prime example of this includes Debian and Fedora, which will employ tools like *apt-get*. In the Debian distribution, to install the apt-get, you would need to initiate the command 'sudo' as a prefix. For example, to install the curl tool, the command statement will be 'sudo apt-get install curl'.

To upgrade the versions of software installed on a distribution, you can use the upgrade command. To balance the upgrade dependencies, click on 'dist-upgrade'. There is a possibility of installing many software programs at the same time. To do this, list the names of the software after a command such as 'goaccess'.

To keep the configuration of software files when trying to uninstall them, use the 'remove' command. The function of the 'purge' command is to completely eradicate the file including any configuration files. If you need only the source file of a software program, use the 'download only source' package option.

ADVANTAGES OF LINUX OVER OTHER OPERATING SYSTEMS

"Linux is the most compatible operating system ever invented." You should be familiar with this phrase by now. Here, we would test the functionality of Linux as compared to other popular operating systems such as Windows. Linux has shortcomings, but its advantages are far more.

Cost

The prices of operating systems that do not offer the kind of services provided by Linux are somewhat ridiculous. After a certain period of time has passed, other operating software will require a fee to upgrade to the next version. A failure to pay this fee will result in a reduction of the operating system's functionality. Microsoft and other operating systems can be licensed only on a particular computer. An attempt to share the OS with another computer will require another fee for licensing. This is unlike Linux, for which a version can be shared on as many computers as possible at no additional charge. All versions of Linux are free except for some advanced versions, which require almost nothing for licensing or upgrading, and the fee is charged only once.

Security

Putting cost aside, let's weigh operating systems, including Linux, on a security scale. The strength of Linux's security outweighs by far those of other operating systems. With Linux, the need to update antivirus versions doesn't exist. The same cannot be said of other operating systems. A Linux program can run for years without being threatened by malware, viruses or worms. The open source of the Linux program makes it possible for any random user to clean the system almost immediately if a virus affects it. With other operating systems, one must wait for the company in charge to provide solutions for the virus.

Choice (Freedom)

As a Linux user, you have the ability to control the operating system in any many ways. Two very essential things you can control are the desktop display and the kernel. In Windows, the default display could overwhelm you and cause you to disrupt the system by trying to install a third-party shell of sorts.

Software

There are hundreds of software programs you can use to complete your major assignments. If you want to alter a command line, you have various options from which to choose. Every day, average users can upgrade the functionality of features that are already available on the Linux program, add new features and improve applications to function more smoothly. What's more, applications or software that come from Linux have more features and functions than any random software. The source code is readily available and almost all of the software is free for installation. In addition, if you are a skilled programmer, you can edit the source code and invent new features according to your own liking. All of this is achievable only in Linux.

Hardware

Linux is suitable for old computers with little or no processing ability and storage. A Linux program that runs on your computer can serve as a firewall or even backup server. Old computers with virtually no RAM will run a Linux program smoothly.

Flexibility

There is no need to worry about anti-piracy gimmicks. When you visit the security forum, you will see that lots of questions are answered and solutions to security problems are provided. You have the option to perform a single AV test, along with other control solutions (SELinux, grsecurity and so on). On other operating systems, there are probably more than 50 AV tests, anti-malware apps, invasion prevention apps and several other security apps that could confuse you.

DISADVANTAGES OF LINUX

Learning

You must be patient when trying to learn the Linux operating system and its functionalities. You must be determined to invest the time that is needed, which may cause you to go beyond your comfort zone. To make this learning process easier, you should seek assistance from those who already have some knowledge and experience with Linux.

Compatibility

While Linux is free, it does have some drawbacks. Linux is deficient when it comes to brand hardware affinity. The kernel contributors and maintainers work assiduously to update the kernel daily. Linux offers little in the way of corporate back-ups unlike other operating systems. You will be lucky to find third-party applications.

Alternative Programs

Even though Linux programmers have done well to create a substitute software for popular operating systems like Windows, some software on Windows cannot be found on

Linux at all. Some of the examples include the Chrome OS, FreeBSD, Syllable, ReactOS and Haik.

ADVANCED UNIX PROGRAMMING VERSUS LINUX

A Linux user talked about her first encounter with UNIX. She came across UNIX while she was still a child in 1972. She was traveling to Bell Labs, which is the place where UNIX was invented. After a long period of time, other coders like herself became very acquainted with the "main stuff," which was known as UNIX. Although Linux also existed then, she was skeptical and didn't believe in Linux. It was probably not the first clone of UNIX she had seen because she published a review of systems with UNIX-like characteristics. It was published in 1985, in an issue of the periodical BYTE magazine. She concluded that in terms of system calls, Coherent was fairly trustworthy even though the commands were not really similar. However, it did not match the industrial strength of typical UNIX III systems.

In the early 1990s, starting from the late 1980s, AT&T-derived UNIX systems were almost everywhere, so clones didn't attract her much. Also, due to the hefty cost of the AT&T hardware, the charges for every single binary code had little or no effect on the overall cost. Just like others, she never knew that Idris and similar clones would disappear eventually.

She next became aware of a similar system when she attended a conference between 1990 and 1991. She met people who were familiar with BSD UNIX, which did not contain codes from AT&T. In that period, the issue was not something run on an almost free Intel base. The primary aim of the GNU was a set of complete operating systems. Not long after that, she stumbled on Linux. Although the name sounded familiar to her, she couldn't remember where she first heard it. All she could remember was that she was desperate to know what Linux was about. At that same time, she was leading research that was being conducted by a group of programmers. Around 1998, the team used Linux in an experiment. She was shocked because the probability of running the Linux program was virtually zero at the time.

Some three years ago, she was toying around with Linux to learn what it was fully about. Coincidentally, she came across Google and still had no idea how good Linux was because she was looking at it from an ordinary user's perspective, not from the stance of a computer programmer.

When she began writing a book in 2002, she decided to go into more detail. She began by sampling the SuSE and FreeBSD programs on two desktop computers. She used a third desktop to run Solaris and yet another desktop to run OSX, which was attached with a Darwin UNIX kernel. The book had almost 19,000 lines of sample codes with almost 300 AT&T UNIX lines.

The results of the test were a surprise. The Linux program she used lagged Solaris in matching the most recent UNIX standard. It lacked system calls like the POSIX inter process communication and the POSIX threads. As she discovered, Linux was well developed, unlike what she had thought when she viewed it from the angle of a user. As she wrote her book, she discovered new things about Linux. The other two test specimens, Darwin and FreeBSD, performed worse than Linux, probably because their development communities were quite small and not well funded.

All of this came about because of Linus Torvald's slight effort to change Minix (a UNIX-inspired educational operating system) into something more exciting. It shows what happens when the right solution collides with the right problem.

When it comes to marketability, Linux has gained a lot of ground because of publications about Microsoft's jitters, SCO's litigation and the Sun's decline. This is the case without even considering the social and domestic benefits of Linux.

Unlike UNIX clones, Linux and most other systems that are BSD-derived have an open source file, so users can manipulate and even develop the file. This means that it is not just the users who can access the source, but also engineers. Computer users can create and improve their kernel without external assistance. Alternatively, they can find distributions and decide to work everything out by themselves, explore the program, learn the ins and outs of the software and make something better out of it.

Even though some operating systems are also open source, Linux requires minimal resources to start or maintain a venture. Well-established software and hardware marketers like HP and IBM depend heavily on SUSE and Arch Linux to survive. Many big Linux users are underground these days so that they can circumvent SCO's radar. Another boost to Linux comes from Walmart, since the company makes money from it.

In fact, Linux could replace UNIX. Both are similar in some ways even if they are not really the same. Perhaps the differences between these software programs can be bridged if the Linux enterprise is modified.

Linux has become more popular among sellers and software users. After the experience with the open source, consumers are now ordering from most of the closed source distributors like Sun, Microsoft, etc. Existing vendors that were initially considered invulnerable are becoming aware of Linux's influence in the consumer market as it threatens to capture corporate desktops.

Linux is a good choice for nations that are still in their developmental stage. It can be used for effectively training their workers, who can acquire and use it without wasting money or running afoul of I.P. agreements between the institution and user.

THE LINUX DEVELOPMENT PROCESS

The OS virtualization technology is systematically used to create several Linux environments on a particular Linux host. Unlike other virtual devices or machines, a Linux container will never permit a strange operating system; instead it fractionizes the kernel of the host OS and also gives a portion of the guest OS to permit the necessary OS functions. No OS is actually faithful, so Linux containers are much more quickly initialized than virtual machines.

Some kernel highlights such as profiles, chroot and CGroups kernel features are being employed by Linux containers to create something similar to a virtual machine. Security modules in Linux allow entrance into the host machine while the container's kernel is being controlled to prevent any form of unauthorized access. What's more, containers can accommodate several Linux versions directly from the operating system of the host provided that the operating system can function simultaneously on the same CPU.

With respect to the various Linux distributions, the Linux container will make available methods of producing container images, an APL for the lifespan, tools that move with the APL, snapshot features, and ways to transfer container instances to different hosts.

HISTORY OF THE CONTAINER

Chroot, a container, was invented in 1979 as the UNIX Chroot. The operating system is almost the same as the UNIX operating system. There is a need to transport the root directory of a process to a new destination on the system that only visible processes can sense because each process needs free space. This feature was included in BSD some three years later.

Woolworth invented one of the first containers in the year 2000. The operating system resembles Chroot except that it contains some new elements and features for separating the filesystem, user and network. It provides a way to identify jails, configuration and installation with an IP address.

"Linux server" is a term that is used to portray a particular jail feature that functions as a fortified parting of resources on the processing unit (the network IP). The parts created and the visual systems are known as "security content" and "virtual private servers," respectively.

The Solaris container was invented in 2004 for special systems and the first version of Solaris was released in 2005. A Solaris container combines various controls and the space created by various zones. These zones work totally within specified limits, which are made up by the boundaries of the operating system.

Open VZ was invented in 2005 and is almost the same as Solaris. It creates visualization and other notable features by using a Linux kernel. Every Open VZ container possesses an abstract file system.

Google initiated a process container to manage resource packages and to collect various processes. As time passed, the name was changed to 'control group' to avoid a situation in which the term 'container' could be confused with a different meaning when the version of the Linux kernel was integrated into another version of the Linux kernel.

LXC is the acronym for 'Linux container' and is a first-generation container manager. It was initiated by using the name space in Linux and stored in an LXC collection of programs. It provided a language script for various APIs. Another important thing to note is that LXC containers will run without patches. Furthermore, Canonical Ltd. funds and supports any project of LXC.

In 2011, Warden was activated by Cloud Foundry. In the process of activation, LXC was employed. After Warden was completely developed, the program was substituted for LXC. Although no strong relationship exists between LXC and Warden, the latter can function on any random operating system that can establish a method of detaching the environment. A daemon can run on Warden, as it makes a provision for a chief API to control containers.

LMCTFY is the acronym for "let me contain that for you". It serves as a provider of app containers, because it is the open source that chips in ideas into the libcontainer. Because of that, no update whatsoever has been made to LMCTFY. Docker kicked off the libcontainer task and now the OCF (Open Container Foundation) has taken control of it.

In the beginning of 2016, Docker usage spread like wildfire. It was recognized on a very large scale. A popular company known as dotCloud actually named Docker and developed it. Just like Warden, Docker borrowed LXC in its beginning stage. As the container grew, LXC was replaced with Docker's own "libcontainer." One importance of Docker is that it provides an environment in which other containers can be managed. The container is composed of an image model that is layered and very efficient. It is essentially a register of different containers, API and so on. Lately, Docker has ventured into producing a container called "Docker Swam" that provides various management options.

CoreOS, in a bid to replicate the Docker container, designed a very similar but much improved container called "Rocket." It was established in 2014. The actual purpose of CoreOS was to design a more secure container than Docker. On the App container, it is regarded as the standard. CoreOS produces other similar containers of the same brand including Docker examples such as CoreOS, flannel, etc.

In 2015, Microsoft took a step toward including a container to assist its system server for apps that are Windows-based. This container is called "Windows container." Although it was not yet released at that time, it was made public with the Windows server in 2016. The execution of the project will make Docker function on Windows without the need for a virtual machine.

THE FUTURE

A few years ago, there was a standard way of transferring containers from virtual machines for software applications. One major reason for undertaking this process was to ensure flexible and cheap prices for the container in comparison to virtual machines. After many years of partnership with Borg and Omega container management, Google successfully implemented container know-how for running Google apps on massive platforms. By getting involved in libcontainer programs and enforcing cgroups, Google successfully enriched the container community. Google has achieved a lot by effectively maximizing container benefits for a very long time. After a while, Microsoft, which lacked VMs on its podium, corrected the deficiency by providing containers on its server.

Due to the fact that they are disclosed to a single point of failure, different containers cannot operate on a single host in a software test setting. The failure of a host will also affect the containers if they are operated altogether on that single host. To circumvent this, a container cluster is used. Google took that initiative and utilized a container cluster called "Kubernetes," which had an open source. Docker, on the other hand, invented a Docker swam solution, which is not yet fully accepted on the ground.

Another remarkable software or program is Microservices, which makes use of containers. A microservice is the simple usage of a web function that can be initiated more quickly than a standard web function. A way to achieve this is by grouping a unit of functionality in a single service and inculcating it into a simple web server.

Thinking deeply about the discussed factors, we can foretell that in some years' time, VMs will be routed out and completely replaced by containers. Some years back, experts worked together to carry out a container solution on the POC stage. However, some of the experts wanted to take the risk by testing them on manufacturing. As clusters develop over time, the current situation will change rapidly.

THE KALI LINUX

Kali Linux is the name given to a Linux distribution whose characteristics include high penetrating testing and security balancing of the Debian Linux type. Kali Linux possesses extensive equipment that is used for protection and security purposes like research, testing and reverse process engineering. The sponsor behind Kali Linux is the prestigious "OFFENSIVE SECURITY," which specializes in information and cyber security.

In March 2013, Kali Linux was officially released in the form a chip of the Debian distribution quality as a replacement for the old Linux "Back Track." As with nearly all Linux versions, Kali Linux is completely free to use for any user. Also, distant wireless support is common among all Linux distributions for wireless links. Kali Linux operates on different hardware and is designed to serve as many wireless networks as possible.

Kali Linux has many different penetrating features that come with it. As an upgraded Back Track version, it comes with new features. Many of the faults and errors that occurred with Back Track have been improved.

Open-source Git tree is a free Windows Git client devoted to the augmenting and improvement of the source codes of the operating system. The development tree is made public for any user who intends to re-structure the program in any way that is needed. Furthermore, the FSH option allows the user to access libraries, files and the help section. Kali Linux strictly conforms to the file system standard.

Many penetration testers will conduct extensive wireless investigations for the inclusion of injection patches in the kernel. Thus, Kali Linux is developed in a fortified and secure atmosphere. The Linux developers are a team of trusted individuals who are familiar with the packages and have access to the site where files are preserved and stored. Every Linux distribution has the signature of its developer or engineer on it. The packages are signed as well.

All penetration tools are originally written in English, although Kali Linux does have multiple-language assistance, allowing users of different languages to work with the software package. Moreover, many users may not be satisfied with the way it was built, so there is an option for users to change the software to their preference, beginning with the kernel.

Kali Linux also possesses ARMEL and ARMHF supports. ARM-based devices that possess single board systems like Black, Raspberry Pi and others are becoming very popular and very expensive. In this regard, Kali Linux's own ARM support will be very extensive so that it can simultaneously work with ARMEL and ARMHF devices. Kali Linux is present on various ARM devices that are inculcated with their mainline distribution features. Because of this, ARM is always upgraded with the distribution.

Kali Linux is specifically designed to satisfy users who are specialized in penetration testing. Penetration testing helps to maximize the use of the Kali Linux program and to protect against attacks. Because Kali Linux was designed to meet the standards of high penetration testing and professional security, many changes have been made to the software. Because of the way Kali Linux was designed to be operated in a single root user setting, several tools that are employed in penetration testing have also been modified.

In terms of disabled network services, Kali Linux has some special features, including hooks that shut down the network services automatically. These hooks permit different installation processes on Kali Linux simultaneously, ensuring that the distributions are protected automatically with respect to whatever is installed on it. Some special services are also automatically included with the software.

INSTALLING KALI LINUX

Installing Kali Linux on your desktop is not difficult. The first thing to do, as usual, is to get a desktop that will accommodate the software. Some systems that can accommodate Kali Linux include AMD64, i386, ARMEL and ARMHF. The necessary hardware is given below. Improved hardware will function better. For instance, the images on the i386 have an automatic kernel so that they can be operated over a memory of four gigabytes. Kali Linux can be copied to a disc, downloaded or transferred by using a Linux drive as the installment medium.

Before you consider installing Linux, you must have the following:

• 20 GB of free space or more for installing the software

• A minimum of 1 GB RAM along with i386 or AMD64 designs

- A CD drive or USB support

Starting the installation process

1. First, successfully download the Kali Linux program.

2. Copy Kali Linux on a disc or ISO.

3. Make sure your system is ready to start from the CD.

Follow the steps below

1. Start with the method you chose in the beginning. The Kali Boot will pop up. Select one of the install options: graphical or text mode. We will choose the GUI install option.

2. Next, select the preferred language option and the location. A list containing several country options will be displayed where you can select your specific country. You'll also be asked to select and configure your keyboard type with the key-map.

3. Confirm your location.

4. Images will automatically be copied to the hard disc. Your network will be scanned, and then you will need to provide a host from your device. For example, we can input KALI LINUX as the name for the host.

5. You can enter a domain name manually or select it by default.

6. Your device will require a non-root user.

7. With all the information you have provided, the program will automatically create an identity account.

8. Adjust the time to that of your geographic zone.

9.   Your system will be investigated and based on this, several options will be displayed. In this example, we will adopt the whole disc instead of the LVM. However, some experts would rather use a manual process for the configuration.

10.   Choose the discs to be partitioned.

11.   Determine whether you wish to secure all your files in a particular partition or separate them into as many partitions as you wish.

12.   Now, the program will ask to go through all of the information you have supplied to check whether you have provided the right information or whether you have made an error that can hinder the functioning of the program. Once you have done that, the information will be permanently saved and there is no going back, so be careful.

13.   In Kali, there is a core registry that disseminates apps. The right address and information must be provided. However, if you choose the NO option, you'll NEVER be able to install from the Kali app registry.

14.   Install Grub.

15.   Lastly, shut down or reboot the system to finish the installation.

You have now completed the installation. You can change the program to produce your results as needed. Below are the testing methodologies you can choose to delve in:

•   Ethical hacking

•   Penetration testing

•   Vulnerability assessment

- Security audits

PROFILING THE WEB SERVER

One of the first steps to take when targeting a company is to put together extensive information from companies without them finding out. The sources of this information are usually internet-based sources. These include the CNN news website, domain name databases (DNS), EDGAR databases and search engines. You can learn more about the company's security measures by following three steps:

1.   **Foot printing**: This step collects information and makes a specific profile of the company's security position. Foot printing uses simple tools to collect data such as administrative and billing information, which includes employee names, emails, addresses and locations. All of this data is easily accessible from the internet.

2.   **Scanning**: During the scanning process, systems that are available and reachable via the internet are detected through port scanning, ping sweeps and operating system identification. The information extracted here involves system architecture and specific IP addresses.

3.   **Enumeration**: This step simply extracts valid accounts from a system using operating-system-specific techniques like routing tables, system banners, user and group names, and SNMP information.

When this is done, the information is passive and no company can detect who is gathering information about it even if they have IDS (Intrusion Detection Software) installed.

In the process of conducting a penetration test, you must gather information, have a detailed map of the target network and conduct a complete assessment. You must also be able to identify each respective system within a network. Information gathering is of two types: passive information gathering and active information gathering.

PASSIVE AND ACTIVE INFORMATION GATHERING

We can define **passive information gathering** as the gathering of information via media that would be hard to trace back to the finder's IP address. It's also called open-source intelligence and works by finding internet-based information. You have access to valuable information that is useful for passive information gathering. It can be used to build maps, understand organizational structures, and assess employees and their relationships with other companies. The information can be found on databases mentioned earlier, like the EDGAR database or archived company information. Since this information is publicly accessible, it's not illegal or unethical to store it. Most databases provide you with tools and resources for accessing this information easily. The homepage of a company is a valuable resource and can be used to reveal sensitive information. The information can be obtained without the company's detection or direct connection. Valuable information like the location of the company, network and system, as well as ownership information, is gathered during passive information gathering. When passive information is being gathered, it is important to collect archived information about systems that are located in the target's network. Different searches are made and the list of searched information includes:

• The target web presence (note: this is not referring only to web pages)

• Search engine information related to the target

• Web groups containing employee or company data

• Personal websites of employees

- Security and exchange data and any additional financial information regarding   the target

- Up-time statistics sites

- Job postings submitted by the target

- Archival sites for additional information

- News groups

- The domain registrar

- Whether the target provides reverse Domain Name System (DNS) information through a third-party service

Active information gathering is the opposite of passive information gathering. Here you gather information by connecting to the target (company). The company is very much aware of your intentions as you gather information with the intention of better understanding the structures and systems that are in place. Active information gathering is not more useful than passive information gathering because there could be a leak in the information that is stored. This could be helpful during penetration testing, which makes active information gathering similar to passive information gathering. This is especially the case when the information is related to the network, as it is not easy to find private information about public archives in the first place.

INVERSE MAPPING

This is a technique that collects information about hosts that are hard to reach using ideas and assumptions to find missing links. Inverse mapping uses RESET scans and obtains information from routers, which provide the internal architecture information of the network. Routers scan for IP addresses and make their decisions based on what is scanned. They provide feedback about addresses that are unreachable.

Routers can be investigated for the IP lists, and the outcome is used to map the targeted network's IP.

Domain Query Answers are sent from the probing computer, which then answers domain questions as a means of extracting the ICMP unreachable messages for a host that doesn't exist.

PORT SCANNING

A port scan is done with two objectives in mind:

1.   To verify the existence of the target systems and to see which of these systems is alive.

2.   To obtain lists of communication channels that can accept connections.

There are four types of port scanning:

A.   Stealth scan

This is a scanning technique that allows you to pass through filtering rules and avoid network traffic. The most popular stealth scan techniques are explicit and are carried out through XMAS scans, NULL scans, SYN/ACK scans and FIN scans.

An XMAS scan, also called the Christmas tree scan, sends TCP packets with FIN, ACK, PST and RST flag sets. The NULL scan uses a TCP packet to turn off all flags as it probes the system to send back a RESET to all of the closed ports. NULL scanning works against most TCP implementations, no matter what operating system it runs on. The SYN/ACK is the first step in a three-way TCP handshake. The TCP identifies the packet as a mistake and sends a RESET to break up connections, which is exactly the right response to detect the existence of a closed port. This is because a SYN/ACK stealth scan ignores the packet if it was from an open port. The FIN scan uses the FIN packet to probe the system of a target port and then waits for its response.

B. TCP connect scan

This scan uses basic TCP connections to establish mechanisms for the interested port on a targeted machine. The scan sends a SYN packet to the specific system and waits to read the type of packet it uses. If the response received is a SYN/ACK packet, the port is in a LISTENING state. If the scan receives a RST/ACK packet, the port is not in a LISTENING state and the connection will RESET. In a case in which a SYN/ACK is received, we can send an ACK. The connection will be terminated when the full connection establishment process has been completed. The only problem is that TCP scans can easily be detected.

C. TCP SYN scan

Also called the half opening scanning, this differs from the TCP connect scan because it does not allow a full connection to be established with the interested port on the target machine. A SYN packet is initiated and sent. If you receive a SYN/ACK packet, it signifies a LISTENING port. If a RST/ACK packet is received, it indicates a Non-Listening port. When a SYN/ACK packet is received, the connection is broken down to RESET. This terminates the TCP handshake and no logs are recorded for the scanning attempts on the site.

D. Proxy scanning/file transfer protocol bounce scanning

In Proxy scanning, the attacker tries to connect to the FTP server with its writable directory, establishes a control communication connection and requests an active data transfer process from the FTP server so that it can send a file across the internet.

PORT SCANNING TECHNIQUES

There are many port scanning techniques but we will discuss only five types:

1) Slow scan
2) Fragmentation scan
3) Random port scan
4) Decoy scan
5) Coordinated scan

The slow scan uses an intrusion detection system to determine if someone with a specific IP address is trying to scan relevant networks. This is called the site detection threshold; the attacking user is usually patient and gives the scan a long time to run through its course.

In a fragmentation scan, all IP packets that carry data are fragmented and information is carried out using a TCP for data fragmentation. This fragmentation links the destination port and the source port with the first packet that was sent. Eight octets of data are usually needed to contain the source and destination port numbers. This pushes the TCP flags into a second fragment, while some intrusion detection systems and filtering devices reassemble during scanning by assuming that the scanned network has already been checked from the access list. Linux is a good example because it has a filtering device on the CONFIG_IP_ALWAYS-DEFRAG kernel option.

The random port scan randomizes the sequences of the port that is probed to prevent detection. It uses a commercial intrusion detection system to search for sequential connection attempts. When a pattern finds a match, the port scan is reported.

Some network scanners are enabled with the decoy feature or with spoofed addresses during an attack. The decoy feature causes an intrusion detection system to assume that the targeted network is undergoing a port scanning by all of the hosts, so that fishing out the real attacker becomes almost impossible. In the past, intrusion detection systems detected decoy hosts by using TTL (Time To Live) field values in their scanned packets. If TTL values were constant, it would seem like they were all factory generated. Another method used to detect a genuine scan among decoys is to trace the route of the originator's IP address. If a non-routable IP address is used, it would lead to denial of service. This can also happen when the IP address belongs to a host that is not live on the network. To prevent this from happening, the attacker uses spoofed IP addresses of the host that is up and running already.

Coordinated scans are used to target single hosts or an entire network. The scans are coordinated when attackers team up to achieve the common goal of trying to get illegal access to a targeted network. When multiple IP addresses probe a targeted network, they all probe from a different machine and at a different time, which makes it almost impossible to detect these scans. A coordinated attack, when carried out properly, is the most effective way to probe a target because it is hardly ever detectable.

Identifying the operating system that runs on a target host/machine is very important because of the many security holes that are operating-system-dependent. Attackers may scan a range of IP addresses for the UDP, TSP ports and its operating system type. When an operating-system-dependent security hole is discovered, the system only needs to go through the list and match the information.

There are many services that can be used to identify operating systems. The most notable is the TELNET service. The second service for identifying an operating system is the DNS HINFO Record, which uses the host's information record to pair strings that identify the host's operating system and the hardware type. DNS HINFO Record is not very effective because it is archaic and as a result, most administrators avoid using it.

Distinct variations in TCP stack implementation are used to determine a remote operating system through the stack fingerprinting technique. The idea behind IP stack fingerprinting lies in the fact that it sends TCP packets to the target IP and waits for a response, which is distinct on various operating systems and varies from one vendor's implementation of the IP stack to another.

TCP stack fingerprinting uses tools like Nmap and Questo. Nmap has a larger database of responses from the operating systems than any other tool. For the most accurate results, an Nmap needs one port opened, at least, at the target's host.

Below are the types of probes and processes used to determine operating system types:

- The fin probe
- The bogus flag probe
- Initial sequence sampling of TCP
- TCP initial window
- ACK value
- ICMP error message quenching
- "Do not fragment bit"
- ICMP message quoting.
- ICMP error message echoing integrity
- Fragmentation handling
- TCP options

1. The FIN probe

To use a FIN probe, we target an open port and send a FIN probe to it. Then, we wait for a reply. Ideally, such a reply would not come. The RFC793 expected behavior ensures that a FIN probe is not responded to. Most stack implementations will react with a RESET. This set of systems includes Windows, CISCO, BSDI, IRIX and HP-UX, and MVS, with a RESET.

2. The bogus flag probe

This type of probe uses a SYN packet with undefined flags and sends the packet to the targeted host. Devices running on the Linux operating system with a kernel prior to 2.0.35 will log the set of flags in the responses they send back. There are, however, operating systems that appear to RESET the connection in the event of the receipt of a SYN+BOGUS probe.

3. TCP initial sequence number sampling

Here, we can search for patterns in the sequence numbers that were initially employed in the implementation of TCP to respond to a linking or connection request.

We can divide this into different groups:

- The traditional 64k (older UNIXs)

- Random increment (such as DG-UX, new versions of Solaris, FreeBSD, IRIX)

- Window boxes that use time-dependent systems (MS Windows)

- True "random" (OpenVMS, Linux, etc.)

4. "Do not fragment bit"

To enhance performance, some operating systems set a "do not fragment bit".

Monitoring this behavior can give the attacker additional information about the targeted operating system.

5. TCP initial window

The initial size of the window for the returned packets of several stack implementations is unique. AIX, for example, remains the only operating system that uses the 0x3F25 value. FreeBSD and OpenBSD use 0x402E.

6. ACK value

In some cases, changes can be made in IP stacks because of a difference in the values that were set in the ACK fields.

For example, suppose you send the message 'FIN|PSH|URG' to the TCP closed port. In most implementations, the ACK in the returned packet is set to be the same as the sequence number received. Windows responds better to an ACK field with the +1 sequence number.

7. ICMP error message quenching

Some operating systems follow the RFC 1812 advice of limiting the sending rate of the various error messages. Only a few operating systems are known to follow this RFC. In the Linux kernel, for instance, the generation of destination unreachable messages is limited to 80 in every second. If this is exceeded, there is a quarter-of-a-second penalty. To test this, a hacker can generate a bunch of packets and send them to several high UDP ports that are chosen randomly. Then, the hacker will count the number of unreachable messages received.

8. ICMP message quoting

An ICMP error message should quote a minute amount of information from the ICMP message that caused the error. The information received is quoted when the message 'PORT UNREACHABLE' is received in the IP header plus eight bytes (IP header+8byte).

9. ICMP error message echoing integrity

When an ICMP error message is sent back, certain stack implementations may intercept the IP header. If an attacker examines the types of alternations that have been made to the headers, the attacker may make certain assumptions about the target operating system.

10. Type of Service (TOS)

In a case whereby the message 'ICMP PORT UNREACHABLE' is sent, the attacker should examine the TOS field. In most implementations, the digit 0 is used for this error. However, in Linux, 0xC0 is always used.

11. Fragmentation handling

When handling overlapping fragments of the IP, the different stack implementations work differently. New portions are used to overwrite the old ones in some cases, while in other cases the reverse is true when the fragments are reassembled.

12. TCP options

All of the hosts do not implement the TCP option. Once you send a query with an option set to a targeted host, this target host will set the option in the reply only if it supports it. One can now test all the options at the same time if one packet is sent that includes all of the options. When the response packet is inspected, you want to check on all of the option fields to see if any of them were set. Some operating systems support all of the advanced options while others support only a few.

THE HACKING GUIDE

As we have discussed in earlier chapters, hacking is a big crime. Whatever is explained or taught in this section is to be used for developmental, educational and research purposes only. We will consider hacking into Android devices, but before then we need to ask some questions. Why are we hacking into an Android device? For what purpose? A vast number of people possess Android devices.

Similar to software development, hacking is difficult and you can't become a professional hacker overnight. Hacking requires great skill and a level of reasoning. As a hacker, your brain must function like a processing unit. To practice hacking on a small platform, you will need to have some experience with one of the various programming languages. Knowledge of programming languages like C++, Linux and FORTRAN is very useful when it comes to hacking. However, you will also need other kinds of knowledge to become a skillful hacker. Daily, by reason of upgrades in security measures, hacking becomes tougher. As a hacker, you must learn to understand and beat security challenges.

PROPERTIES OF KALI LINUX 2.0

If you are a pro at penetrating servers and breaking into networks, the easiest way to go about your business is by harnessing the power of Kali Linux 2.0. Kali Linux 2.0 is by far the best Linux distribution that makes hacking very easy for the programmer. You will be able to achieve your goals in little time and become the owner of your personal network.

The most important features of Kali Linux are mentioned below:

1. Metasploit

Metasploit is a frame that helps to create exploits, shellcodes, triggers, honey pots and payloads. Metasploit is a bank of several exploits and similar elements that are packed into its frame. The software is public and can be used on many operating systems out there, including Linux and Windows. It comes with Kali Linux by default. Metasploit is a foul device that can threaten other networks. You want to examine faults in network security and learn how to manage them to prevent external attacks.

Web applications and servers are also subject to attacks by Metasploit. In Metasploit, GUI and command line interfaces exist equally. Metasploit is available as a free version and but also has paid version (Metasploit Pro), which offers more functionality.

2. NMAP

NMAP is short for "network mapper." It probes a network while searching for ports that are accessible to map network servers and so on. The core function of NMAP is security analysis and the examination of networks to detect computers that are available online. NMAP uses IP addresses and packets in a way that reveals useful details about a network. For example, it shows the ports that can be used to access the network and the apps being used on the computer. It is advisable to first have some idea concerning the commands before proceeding further to the GUI.

3. Armitage

The Armitage is a display control tool employed in cyber security that creates an interface for the Metasploit attachment that simplifies Metasploit, making it less complex so it can easily be comprehended. Armitage is a good place to start if you want to learn more about Metasploit. All of the functions of Metasploit are gathered by Armitage in the procedures of hacking, as they are meant to exploit, circumvent and raid a network.

4. Jhon the Ripper

JTC is the acronym for "Jhon the Ripper." It is a renowned tool for breaking through an arena that is heavily secured with passwords. Simply referred to as Jhon in the hacking world, it is the primary tool used to launch what is called a dictionary intrusion. Jhon the Ripper has a bank of text called the "word list", which is composed of previously cracked passwords. Jhon the Ripper selects one of these passwords from its bank and replaces the wordlist of the password to be cracked. Then it gives the result of the new imputed password. In other words, the hacker takes a previously cracked password and interferes with the system in such a way that this previously cracked password is substituted for the password to be cracked. After that, the past success is re-initiated by Jhon and the substituted password is re-cracked. There is a similarity between Jhon the Ripper and THC Hydra, which is a similar cracking tool. The slight difference is that Jhon is used offline while Hydra is used an online.

5. Wireshark

Wireshark is an open source tool that scrutinizes networks with an outline of network traffic. This tool belongs to the category of network sniffers.

Ethereal was Wireshark's old name. Its core function is to keep an eye on differences that are used to monitor network traffic and to investigate packets that are sent to and fro. After all of this, the results are presented to the user in a format that can be understood. As time has passed, there have been noticeable advancements. For example, filters and other various packets like color coding have been created. All of this development has helped in one way or another, especially in sharpening the penetrating power of the testers. These testers are able to penetrate further into networks and thoroughly scrutinize the packets.

If you really want to become a master in network analysis, network penetration and acquire other hacking skills, you must have experience and knowledge about Wireshark.

6. THC Hydra

Hydra, very identical to Jhon, is a password-dismantling device. In the hands of expert hackers, Hydra can be dangerous. It is mostly combined with Jhon, as both are used simultaneously. Hydra breaks passwords by combining the power of a dictionary and brute force to assault a password where it is to be imputed. Hydra gives permission to a large scope of protocols. Examples include SSH, POP3, IMAP,

Database, SMB, VNC, LDAP, SMB, RTPS, HTTP, POP, TCP, SMTP and RTPS.

The most powerful tool that currently exists online is "Suite." Suite is an app that provides web services and penetration testing. When it is fully maximized, the possibility of its usage is almost limitless. Below are some of the features of the Burp Suite.

Intercepting Proxy is a feature that monitors and improves communication between an application and the web browser.

Spider is a feature that specifies all lists, names and characteristics of files that exist on a network.

Web Scanner is an important feature that scans for loopholes in the server.

Intruder is a feature that can be used to launch attacks against networks. It is used to scan for flaws and take advantage of them.

Repeater improves and makes solicitations on behalf of the user.

Sequencer examines the irregularity of the token's CSRF, authenticity token, etc.

Extensions allow the user to include his or her own customized plugin or to install plugins directly from the systems database. They are used to creatively stage a tactical and cryptic attack.

7. OWASP Zed

One characteristic of the OSWAP Zed Attack Proxy (acronym: ZAP) is that it has no price tag attached to it. Its open source is made available to the public. OSWAP is a popular feature and an effective proxy tool that can substitute the Burp Suite. OSWAP is user friendly and does its job efficiently and effectively because it exposes the flaws of web apps. The functions of OSWAP are summarized as follows:

A. Manual testing

B. Scrutinizing networks for leakages

C. Scrutinizing the user target

8. Engineering Toolkit

The Social-Engineering Toolkit, or SET as it is called, is another important thing to mention. With this tool, assaults are launched against the user who is operating the system instead of the system itself. It has some special attributes that grant access to Java applets. The user is not aware of these applets because the SET ensures everything is done underground. This command line, when maximized, can produce effective results. It works on any basic operating system including Linux and Windows.

9. Aircrack-ng

This is another kit that dissembles passwords and allows users to access the internet. In the right hands, it can be a profitable tool. However, it is difficult and requires a lot of effort. For newbies, Aircrack-ng is a shortwave cracking program. It is an 802.11 WEP and WPA-PSK keys cracking kit that can reclaim keys from various kinds of data. However, the data must have adequate packets and be trapped (in monitor mode). Aircrack-ng is an indispensable tool that you definitely want to be using.

Novices should be able crack a secured WEP with the right tools. However, a lot of effort will be required to crack a WPA/WPA2.

BASIC PORT SCANNING TECHNIQUES YOU NEED TO KNOW

Port scanning is a procedure that aims to analyze the open ports of a computer system with the help of special tools. To carry out this scanning, it is not necessary to register on the target system as you must only be connected to it through a local network. With the help of port scanners, special data packets are sent to the different ports and the corresponding error messages or messages are analyzed and evaluated by the tool. Regardless of the functionality of the port scanning program being used, information can be obtained not only about which ports are open or closed, but also about the operating system that is being used by the target computer. Furthermore, port scanning can also tell you about the services or applications that are using the corresponding ports.

Port scanning is a very efficient way for system administrators to control data traffic in networks and to filter out their potential weaknesses. In some cases, specific network problems can also be solved. Because the tools do not have a significant influence on the performance capacity of the systems being examined, they can be used without hesitation for such security measures. In a domestic atmosphere, the ports are automatically opened, provided that the firewall does not prevent them. Port scanning helps maintain an overview and shows ports that are no longer needed. These ports can then be closed to minimize risks that may affect security.

How exactly does port scanning work?

There are many different methods that are used to scan ports, most of which revolve around the TCP connection protocol. To understand the basic processes that occur in port scanning, it is important to understand how a TCP protocol connection is established.

1. Within the framework of a process called the three-way handshake, the client first sends a SYN (synchronize) packet to the corresponding destination port.
2. If it reaches an application, it receives a SYN / ACK packet (synchronize acknowledge = "confirm synchronization") that confirms the connection.
3. The client responds in the third and final step with an ACK (acknowledge = "confirm") package, after which the connection is established and data exchange is initiated.
4. If the contact is established with a closed port, the client receives a packet with the flag RST (reset = "reset") in response. Thus, negotiation is interrupted.

Since data exchange with the various applications would be very costly and very complex, the port scanner is limited to a simple connection attempt, as shown by the scanning methods that are mentioned below.

TCP SYN

In the case of TCP SYN, it is possible to speak of an average open scanning, since it does not aim to establish a complete TCP connection. In this mode, typical SYN packets can be sent to each of the ports with the port scanner, after which a response from the destination host is expected. If the host responds with a SYN / ACK packet, the corresponding port becomes open and the connection can be established. If the response consists of an RST packet, the port remains closed. If the destination host has not yet sent a response, a packet filter such as a firewall has interfered in the process. TCP SYN scans are not visible to the reviewed applications and therefore do not generate log data. Hence, they are also called "stealth scans."

TCP Connect

If you are using your port scanner to carry out a connect-type process, you are not generating or sending the data packets, but you are calling the connect system instead. This "calling" is available on almost all operating systems. Also, the web browser uses calling to establish a connection to a server. This scanning tool is not involved in establishing the connection, but is the operating system for the person in charge of it. The person can either (1) create a successful connection and confirm that the port is open, or (2) fail in the attempt and indicate that the corresponding port is closed. If the connection is established completely, it is easy to see (in the log files of applications with open ports) whether this polling method was used. However, if you lack the rights to send raw data packets, the TCP connect method can be a useful alternative to SYN scanning.

TCP FIN, Xmas and Null

With these three methods of port scanning, you can also differentiate between open and closed ports. For this, the two basic principles registered in the RFC (Request for Comments) of TCP (793) can be applied. On the one hand, a closed port must always respond to incoming packets other than RST packets. On the other hand, the open port must ignore all packages not marked as SYN, RST or ACK. These three methods behave exactly the same way. The test packets that are sent are taken care of because of the RFC provisions; a closed port responds with an RST packet and an open port does not show any reaction on its part. However, because only some routers transmit error messages when a port is filtered, there may also be a non-response in the case of a filtered port. Although these procedures are more discrete than SYN scans, they have the disadvantage of not working when systems do not strictly conform to the RFC 793 protocol. Windows would be the most important representative in this case.

UDP

UDP headers are sent empty and out of data UDP headers to all target ports. If a service responds with a UDP packet, the port belonging to it is open. If the router sends the port scanner error message "Port unreachable" (Type 3, Code 3), the port is closed. Other types of error messages report that a packet filter blocks the port. The big problem that comes with scanning ports with UDP is that it takes a lot of time, as in many systems the task of issuing the corresponding error messages can be lengthy for security reasons, and open ports respond very irregularly. The Linux kernel limits the number of messages to, say, one per second, which means you can scan 65,535 ports in about 18 hours.

Uses of a Port Scanner

Security scanners are very useful tools for system administrators and network administrators because they can used to monitor security. On the other hand, a port scanner is sometimes used by hackers to breach a system. However, port scanners are not considered to be from the direct hacking tools because they are not used to attack a system directly. Rather, they are used to gather information before an attack is launched.

HOW TO IDENTIFY YOUR OPERATING SYSTEM (OS)

The operating system is one of the most important software programs on a computer. Operating systems execute elementary tasks such as sending information to the screen, recognizing the keyboard connection, keeping track of directories and files on the disk, and monitoring external devices such as scanners, printers, etc. The operating system is also used to protect and secure the system, preventing unauthorized users from gaining access. There are different kinds of operating systems, which are explained below.

SINGLE-USER

Single-user operating systems are those that support only one user at a time, regardless of the number of processors the computer has or the number of processes or tasks the user can execute at the same time. Personal computers typically have this kind of operating system.

MULTI-USERS:

Multi-user operating systems are capable of servicing more than one user at a time. They will either use several terminals that will be connected to the computer through remote sessions in a communications network, or through the number of processors in the machine that each user can execute simultaneously.

MONO TASKS:

Mono tasks systems are those that allow only one task to be completed at a time by the user. This may be the case in a multi-user and single-task system, in which multiple users are allowed at the same time but each can complete only one task at a time.

NETWORK OPERATING SYSTEM

A network operating system (NOS) is software that allows the interconnection of computers to access services, resources, hardware and software. This essentially creates a computer network. Just as a computer cannot work without an operating system, a computer network cannot function without a network operating system. It consists of software that makes it possible for a computer system to communicate with other computers in a network environment.

OPERATING SYSTEM NETWORK PROCESSORS

A free operating system, according to the Free Software Foundation, offers four types of freedoms. It allows you to:

1. Run the program to perform any activity you want without restrictions.

2. Study the operation of the program and modify it according to your needs.

3. Redistribute copies of the program.

4. Improve the program and distribute copies of the modifications.

Types of Operating Systems

The OS awakens the computer and causes it to recognize the CPU, memory, keystroke, video system and disk drives. In addition, it provides the facility for users to communicate with the computer and serves as a platform from which to run application programs. The most popular operating systems are mentioned below.

1) **DOS:** The famous DOS, which stands for Disk Operating System, is best known by the names PC-DOS and MS-DOS. MS-DOS was created by Microsoft and is essentially the same OS as PC-DOS.

The reason for its continued popularity is the overwhelming volume of available software and the installed base of Intel-based computers. When Intel released the 80286, DOS became so popular that DOS and its applications represented most of the PC software market. At that time, IBM compatibility became a necessity for products to succeed. Even with the new operating systems that have hit the market, DOS is still a solid contender among the various operating software that are available today.

2) **Windows 3.1:** Microsoft decided to create an operating system that had a user-friendly graphical interface and the result was Windows. This system displayed icons on the screen that represented different files or programs, which could be

accessed by double clicking with the mouse. All of the applications created for Windows looked alike, so it was easy to learn how to use new software once someone had learned the basics.

3) **Windows 95:** In 1995, Microsoft introduced a new and improved version of Windows 3.1. Improvements to this OS included multitasking support and 32-bit architecture, which allowed the user to run better applications and improve efficiency.

4) **Windows NT:** This version of Windows specialized in networks and servers. With this OS, the users could interact effectively between two or more computers.

5) **OS/2:** This OS was created by IBM. It has 32-bit support and its interface is very good. The problem with this operating system is that it has not received the support it deserves in terms of applications. That is, many applications have not been created to take advantage of the features of the OS, as most of the software market has been monopolized by Windows.

6) **Mac OS:** Macintosh computers would not be as popular as they are if they did not have Mac OS as the plant operating system. This operating system is so user friendly that anyone can use it in a very short time. It is also great for organizing files and using them effectively. This was created by Apple.

7) **UNIX:** The UNIX operating system was created by AT&T's Bell Labs in 1969 and is now one of the pillars of the information highway. UNIX is a multi-user and multitasking OS, which runs on different computers, including supercomputers, mainframes, minicomputers, personal computers and workstations. This means many users can use the same computer through terminals.

Kali is the dream of upcoming hackers, who know that it will solve a lot of their problems. Kali is wired up with orderly designed equipment that is easy to operate. However, there are still other operating systems that match its quality.

FEATURES OF PARROT SECURITY OS

Just like Kali, the Parrot security operating system is Debian-derived and is used generally for penetration testing, forensics and other purposes. Released some four years ago, it has been extensively developed and has many exciting attributes.

- Parrot Home is a feature of Parrot that is meant to assist users, giving them access to the beautiful atmosphere of Debian and exposing them to the inbuilt penetration testing tools. It also provides assistance in terms of how they can be effectively used.

- The Parrot Air attribute is employed mainly in the wireless system of penetration testing.

- The Parrot Studio attribute focuses on multimedia creation functions.

- The Parrot Cloud attribute operates on a VPS and jump box. It is aimed at apps that deal with servers and enables the user to access the full package of penetration test kits excluding the front-end graphics.

- The Parrot IOT attribute was built for systems that have low resources such as the Pine64, Raspberry Pi and Orange Pi systems.

- The Parrot Security attribute, being the real Parrot OS, was designed with privacy in mind. Its design also favors forensics, penetration testing and future developments. Attention hasn't shifted from the original distribution and purpose, even if it doesn't really have a wide range of functions. With several security features, the program is a desktop force that has the requirements for successful penetration. It makes hacking what it is.

Users of Kali will also find Parrot indispensable for their work. As with Kali, you'll feel very much at home with Parrot, and you won't need to re-learn the basics of flowing with the operating system.

Step 1: Install the Parrot Security OS.

First, we need to download an OS called Parrot Security ISO. You can probably get it on Parrot Security's official website along with the ISO's hashes. After a successful download, the hash should be confirmed. If the hash is not of the same type as the ISO, the file is affected and is not valid. A good idea would be to visit the Parrot site and download the most recent version. Confirming the hash is a simple process. For the hash to be verified on Windows, open the run wizard by pressing the WIN+R and then type **CMD** into the dialog box. Hit enter. When the command prompt opens, type the code **certutil**.

"certutil-hashfile Parrot-full-3.8_amd_64 SHA1" - if your version is 3.8.

For hash confirmation in a Mac operating system, start the command line and execute the code - **shasum Parrot-full-3.8_amd_64.ova**.

For confirmation on Linux, input the code **sha1sum**.

Should the hash correlate, you're free to proceed to the following stage.

Step 2 : Create a Virtual Machine.

To run the operating system, we need to test it on a random machine. First, you'll need to copy the image on a drive and then start the system. While this method works, it requires a lot of time. The new devices can successfully run Linux's Guest software. As a result, virtualization will become more engaging. What's more, we can do away with the device if it poses a lot of problems.

We will make use of a VirtualBox on a Windows operating system that is detached from the VirtualBox site. (VirtualBox is a strong virtualization and highly efficient tool that comes with an open-source license under GNU.) If properly done, the procedure ought to operate on all significant platforms available.

During the installation, you can experiment with a live disc rather than a virtual disc. After you kickstart VirtualBox, the manager will pop up immediately.

There will be a Parrot system open on the system. If you need to restart or run another one, scroll to the left corner to do so. Input the name of your machine of choice and click on Linux. After this, some versions will be provided. Choose Debian but make sure that the version is suitable for your system. Choose either a 32 or 64-bit version and make sure that there is enough space on your disc.

CONCLUSION

Thank you again for purchasing this book!

I hope this book was able to help you learn more about hacking. The next section is about the various online resources that you can use and learn from.

Finally, if you enjoyed this book, then I'd like to ask you for a favor. Would you be kind enough to leave a review for this book on Amazon? It'd be greatly appreciated!

Good luck!

APPENDIX A: WIRELESS HACKING RESOURCES

With the rate at which technology is improving, especially in the wireless network niche, you need to keep yourself and your company safe by staying up to date on developing standards and tools. Although this book has walked you through various techniques for hacking and protecting yourself, there is still a lot to learn as time goes by. Below are some of the resources you can use to learn more.

CERTIFICATIONS

We have covered ethical hacking in this book, and we think this is one of the best tests you can take to see how knowledgeable you are. The following are the two organizations that certify individuals:

➢ **Certified Wireless Network Professional Program: www.cwnp.com/**

➢ **Certified Ethical Hacker: www.eccouncil.org/CEH.htm/**

General Resources

According to research, the Internet is something almost 90 percent of people can't do without daily. Everyone browses, everyone wants a Facebook account. The internet is a valuable resource. However, using the internet is like trying to get a sip of water from a firehose. You must stem the flow of information. We have compiled a list of sites that provide vital information about wireless networks on a regular basis. Plus, you can subscribe to their free email lists.

➢ **SearchNetworking.com: www.searchnetworking.com**

➢ **SearchSecurity.com: www.searchsecurity.com/**

- ➢ **SearchMobileComputing.com:**
  www.searchmobilecomputing.com/

HACKER STUFF

As we have stressed in other chapters, if you want to catch an enemy, you need to think like an enemy. The same applies to a thief. In *The Art of War*, Sun Tzu writes that you need to understand your enemy to defeat him/her. This relates back to the methodology that learning about your enemy is an excellent tactic. You need to understand your enemy, think like him and act like him because if you can really put yourself in your enemy's mindset, you will be able to understand him/her better. We have compiled for you the best sites that will help you better understand crackers and hackers.

- ➢ **Honeypots: Tracking Hackers: www.tracking-hackers.com**

- ➢ **The Hacker Quarterly magazine: www.2600.com**

- ➢ **Computer Underground Digest: www.soci.niu.edu/~cudigest**

- ➢ **The Online Hacker Jargon File: www.jargon.8hz.com**

- ➢ **PHRACK: www.phrack.org**

- ➢ **Hacker t-shirts and other equipment: www.thinkgeek.com**

WIRELESS ORGANIZATIONS

There are many wireless organizations out there, but two of them are: Wi-Fi Alliance and IEEE.

IEEE (Institute of Electrical and Electronics Engineers)

In this book, we have mentioned wireless standards like 802.11, 802.11a, 802.11b, 802.11g and 802.11i. These standards are implemented by the IEEE (**www.ieee.org**). The Institute of Electrical and Electronics Engineers (IEEE) has been in operation for decades and is known for developing open wireless standards for Wireless Local Area Networks (LANs), Wireless Metropolitan Area Networks (MANs) and Wireless Personal Area Networks (PANs). You can differentiate the 802.11 standards ("Over the air") from the 802.3 Ethernet standards ("Over the wire"). You can read more about IEEE standards by visiting previous chapters or consulting Internet blogs and forums.

Wi-Fi Alliance

This organization was formerly known as WECA and was formed in 1999. The Wi-Fi Alliance (**www.wifialliance.com**) started as a non-profit organization that certified the interoperability of all wireless LAN products based on IEEE 802.11 specifications. This company is very large now, as it has more than 200 subsidiaries from around the globe. Plus, it has more than 1,000 certified devices.

LOCAL WIRELESS GROUPS

Facebook is controlled by a group of people because a single person cannot do everything alone. Have you been thinking about how to get serious with wireless ethical hacking? If your answer is yes, you need to immerse yourself in the culture. You need to hook yourself up with people who are wireless aficionados; people who can introduce you to new tools, useful whitepapers and other resources. Wireless organizations are springing up like crabgrass and enabling individuals to meet likeminded people. Following are some of the wireless user groups you can start with:

- Corkwireless, Cork, Cork County, IE: **www.corkwireless.com/**

- Georgia Wireless User Group, Atlanta, GA, US. **www.gawug.com**

- Green Bay Professional Packet Radio, Green Bay, WI, US: **www.qsl.net/n9zia/**

- Houston Wireless, Houston, TX, US: **www.houstonwireless.org**

- IrishWAN, IE: **www.irishwan.org/**

- Longmount Community Wireless Project, Longmount, CO, US: **http://long-wire.net/**

- Madrid Wireless, Madrid, Madrid, ES: **http://madridwireless.net/**

- Marin Unwired, Marin County, CA, US: **www.digiville.com/wifi-marin/index.htm**

- NoCatNet, Sonoma County, CA, US: **http://nocat.net**

- NYCWireless, New York City, NY, US: **http://nycwireless.net**

- NZ Wireless, Auckland, NZ: **www.nzwireless.org/**

- Orange County California Wireless Users Group, Brea, CA, US: **www.occalwug.org/**

- Personal Telco, Portland, OR, US: **www.personaltelco.net**

- Rooftops, Boston/Cambridge, MA, US: **http://rooftops.media.mit.edu/**

- Salt Lake Area Wireless Users Group (SLWUG), Salt Lake City, UT, US: **www.saltlakewireless.net/**

- San Diego Wireless Users Group, San Diego, CA, US: **www.sdwug.org**

- Seattle Wireless, Seattle, WA, US: **www.seattlewireless.net**

- Southern California Wireless Users Group, Southern California, CA, US: **www.socalwug.org**

- StockholmOpen.net, Stockholm, SE: **www.stockholmopen.net/index.php**

- The Toronto Wireless User Group (TorWUG), Toronto, ON, CA: **www.torwug.org/**

- Tri-Valley Wireless Users Group, US: **www.tvwug.org**

- Xnet Wireless, Mornington, AU: **www.x.net.au/**

- WiFi Ecademy, London, England, UK: **www.wifi.ecademy.com/**

- Wireless Technology Forum, Atlanta, GA, US: **www.wirelesstechnologyforum.com**

- Wireless France, FR: **www.wireless-fr.org/spip/**

If your location isn't on the list above, you can try the following alternatives to find a user group near you:

- **www.practicallynetworked.com/tools/wireless_articles_community.htm**

- **www.wirelessanarchy.com/#Community%20Groups**

- **www.personaltelco.net/index.cgi/WirelessCommunities**

SECURITY AWARENESS AND TRAINING

Some things are naturally easy to avoid. Take, for instance, getting management or staff to pay attention to information security; this is not an easy task. Some companies will take care of such things for you and help you get the message across to your organization:

➢ Greenidea, Inc. Visible Statement: **www.greenidea.com**

➢ The Security Awareness Company: **www.thesecurityawarenesscompany.com**

➢ Security Awareness, Inc. Awareness Resources: **www.securityawareness.com**

➢ U.S. Security Awareness: **www.ussecurityawareness.org**

WIRELESS TOOLS

The wireless sections in this book have many details about wireless tools. We have described numerous tools that can be used in wireless networks. Most of the tools mentioned above were summarized and classified, and information was provided about where to get them. However, in case you are just starting out, the tools we will mention in this section will make for a nice shopping list.

Have you ever heard the term "cross-platform"? This refers to programs that have the ability to work on any kind of computer regardless of the type of OS on the system. All tools are placed in the category, which defines what they do. However, among all these tools, there are some that defy categorization. Instead of ignoring these excellent tools, we have made the following list:

➢ BLADE Software IDS Informer: **www.bladesoftware.net**

➢ Foundstone SiteDigger Google query tool:
www.foundstone.com/resources/freetools.htm

➢ MAC-address-vendor lookup: **http://coffer.com/mac_find**

> SMAC MAC-address editor for Windows: **www.klcconsulting.net/smac/**

> WiGLE database: **www.wigle.net/gps/gps/GPSDB/query/**

> WiFimaps: **www.wifimaps.com**

VULNERABILITY DATABASES

You obviously can't solve a problem without knowing its origin, and you can't stay protected if you are not taking security measures yourself. As an ethical hacker, you must understand the vulnerabilities or weaknesses associated with your software or hardware. When you engage in the planning process, the information you receive will determine the type of tests you will perform on your system. Some of the vulnerability databases are:

> US-CERT Vulnerability Notes Database: **www.kb.cert.org/vuls**

> NIST ICAT Metabase: **http://icat.nist.gov/icat.cfm**

> Common Vulnerabilities and Exposures: **http://cve.mitre.org/cve**

LINUX DISTRIBUTIONS

As famous as the Windows operating system is, it is not the best OS for some wireless testing tools. When we want to talk about the best operating systems out there, we can look at LINUX, UNIX or BSD. Many wireless testing tools operate perfectly on these operating systems. This means you need to familiarize yourself with not just Windows but also these other operating systems. As a Linux user, you can purchase a commercial product like Red Hat Linux or SuSe. The only problem is that it is overkill for your purposes. Instead of purchasing those tools, why not try the free Linux distributions? Below is a list of distributions you can use for free:

- ➢ Auditor: **http://new.remote-exploit.org/index.php/Auditor_main**
- ➢ Cool Linux CD: **http://sourceforge.net/project/showfiles.php?group_id=55396&release_id=123430**
- ➢ DSL (Damn Small Linux): **www.damnsmalllinux.org/**
- ➢ GNU/Debian Linux: **www.debian.org/**
- ➢ KNOPPIX: **www.knoppix.net/get.php**
- ➢ SLAX: **http://slax.linux-live.org/**
- ➢ WarLinux: **http://sourceforge.net/projects/warlinux/**

SOFTWARE EMULATORS

Have you ever thought about using two different operating systems on one computer system at the same time? Or pasting from one OS to another? If you have wondered how things like this are done, consider a software emulation product. Some call it partitioning. Below is a list of companies known for software emulation products:

- ➢ Bochs: **http://bochs.sourceforge.net/**
- ➢ Cygwin: **http://cygwin.com/**
- ➢ DOSEMU: **www.dosemu.org/**
- ➢ Microsoft Virtual PC: **www.microsoft.com/mac/products/virtualpc/virtualpc.aspx?pid=virtualpc**
- ➢ Plex86: **http://savannah.nongnu.org/projects/plex86/**
- ➢ Vmware: **www.vmware.com/**
- ➢ WINE: **www.winehq.com/**

- Win4lin: **www.netraverse.com/**

RF PREDICTION SOFTWARE

The radio frequency prediction software helps you simulate the radiation pattern of an AP without having to physically install one. As a tester, you can use the exact software you need to predict wherever you may find a signal. Following are three such programs you can use:

- Airespace:
  www.airespace.com/products/AS_ACS_location_ tracking.php

- Alcatel:
  www.ind.alcatel.com/products/index.cfm?cnt=omnivi sta_acs_locationtrack

- Radioplan:
  www.electronicstalk.com/news/rop/rop100.html

RF Monitoring

Humans create machines, but a machine's results can be more accurate than those of humans. Monitoring a signal strength yourself without any tools can be very difficult. This is why you need a tool to help you test signal strength and bit error rate. Although we have already mentioned some tools you can use to monitor signal strength, such as Kismet or NetStumbler, their results are not as accurate as those of the following tools:

- aphunter:
  www.math.ucla.edu/~jimc/mathnet_d/download.htm l

- E-Wireless: **www.bitshift.org/wireless.shtml**

- Gkrellm wireless plug-in: http://gkrellm.luon.net/gkrellm wireless.phtml

- Gnome Wireless Applet: **http://freshmeat.net/projects/gwifiapplet/**

- Gtk-Womitor: **www.zevv.nl/wmifinfo/**

- GWireless: **http://gwifiapplet.sourceforge.net/**

- Kifi: **http://kifi.staticmethod.net/**

- KOrinoco: **http://korinoco.sourceforge.net/**

- KWaveControl: **http://kwavecontrol.sourceforge.net/**

- KWiFiManager: **http://kwifimanager.sourceforge.net/**

- Linux Wireless Extensions: **http://pcmciacs.sourceforge.net/ftp/contrib/**

- Mobydik.tk: **www.cavone.com/services/mobydik_tk.aspx**

- NetworkControl: **www.arachnoid.com/NetworkControl/index.html**

- NetworkManager: **http://people.redhat.com/dcbw/Network Manager/**

- Qwireless: **www.uv-ac.de/qwireless/**

- Wavemon: **www.janmorgenstern.de/wavemon-current.tar.gz**

- WaveSelect: **www.kde-apps.org/content/show.php?content=19152**

- Wimon: **http://imil.net/wimon/**

- Wmap: **www.datenspuren.org/wmap**

- wmifinfo: **www.zevv.nl/wmifinfo/**

- WMWave: **www.schuermann.org/~dockapps/**

- WmWiFi: **http://wmwifi.digitalssg.net/?sec=1**

- Wscan:
  www.handhelds.org/download/packages/wscan/

- wvlanmon:
  http://file.wankota.org/program/linux/wavelan/

- XNetworkStrength:
  http://gabriel.bigdam.net/home/xnetstrength/

- xosview: **http://open-linux.de/index.html.en**

ANTENNAE

An antenna can help you broadcast signals, but can also cost a lot of money. We understand that you are working on a budget and, therefore, you shouldn't spend all your money on an antenna. The beauty is that you can build a custom antenna or purchase one for a reasonable amount of money. We have found some sites that offer economical antennae you can use for your ethical hacking work. The sites are:

- Cantenna: **www.cantenna.com**

- Hugh Pepper's cantennas, pigtails and supplies:
  http://home.comast.net/~hughpep

- Making a wireless antenna from a Pringles can:
  www.oreillynet.com/cs/weblog/view/wlg/448

And at the same time, you can find an excellent reference page for antennae at: **www.wardrive.net/general/antenna**

WARDRIVING

According to Wikipedia, wardriving is the act of searching for Wi-Fi networks by a person who is in a moving vehicle, using a smartphone or a laptop. It can be a handy tool for your wireless ethical hacking kit. Luckily, numerous tools are available. They are:

- Aerosol: **www.sec33.com/sniph/aerosol.php**
- Airscanner: **www.snapfiles.com/get/pocketpc/airscanner.html**
- AP Scanner: **www.macupdate.com/info.php/id/5726**
- AirMagnet: **https://goo.gl/AXf4jL**
- AP Radar: **http://apradar.sourceforge.net**
- Apsniff: **www.monolith81.de/mirrors/index.php?path=apsniff/**
- BSD-Airtools: **www.dachboden.com/projects/bsd-airtools.html**
- dstumbler: **www.dachboden.com/projects/dstumbler.html**
- gtk-scanner: **http://sourceforge.net/projects/wavelan-tools**
- gWireless: **http://gwifiapplet.sourceforge.net/**
- AiroPeek: **http://www.wildpackets.com/products/airopeek**
- iStumbler: **http://istumbler.net/**
- KisMAC: **https://goo.gl/rxgCUY**
- MacStumbler: **www.macstumbler.com/**
- MiniStumbler: **www.netstumbler.com/downloads/**
- Mognet: **www.lot3k.net/tools/Wireless/Mognet-1.16.tar.gz**

- NetChaser: **www.bitsnbolts.com**

- Network Stumbler: **www.netstumbler.com/downloads**

- perlskan: **http://sourceforge.net/projects/wavelan-tools**

- PocketWarrior: **www.pocketwarrior.org/**

- Kismet: **https://goo.gl/wLGz6U**

- pocketWinc: **www.cirond.com/pocketwinc.php**

- Prismstumbler: **http://prismstumbler.sourceforge.net**

- Sniff-em: **www.sniff-em.com**

- Sniffer Wireless: **www.networkgeneral.com/**

- StumbVerter: **www.michiganwireless.org/tools/Stumbverter/**

- THC-Scan: **www.thc.org/releases.php?q=scan**

- THC-WarDrive: **www.thc.org/releases.php?q=wardrive**

- WarGlue: **www.lostboxen.net/warglue/**

- WarKizniz: **www.michiganwireless.org/tools/WarKizNiz/**

- Wellenreiter: **www.wellenreiter.net/**

- Wi-Scan: **www.michiganwireless.org/tools/wi-scan/**

- WiStumbler: **www.gongon.com/persons/iseki/wistumbler/index.html**

- Wireless Security Auditor: **www.research.ibm.com/gsal/wsa/**

- Wlandump: **www.guerrilla.net/gnet_linux_software.html**

WIRELESS IDS/IPS VENDORS

Consider this a kind of protection for wireless users. Wireless IDS/IPS products are very important. We have listed some IDS/IPS products for you below:

- AirDefense: **www.airdefense.net**

- AirMagnet: **www.airmagnet.com**

- BlueSocket: www.bluesocket.com

- ManageEngine: **http://origin.manageengine.adventnct.com/products/wifi-manager**

- NetMotion Wireless: **www.netmotionwireless.com**

- Red-Detect: **www.red-m.com/Products/Red-Detect**

- Senforce Wi-Fi Security: **www.senforce.com/entwirelessecur.htm**

- Vigilant Minds: **www.vigilantminds.com**

- WiFi Manager: **http://manageengine.adventnet.com/products/wifi-manager/index.html**

WIRELESS SNIFFERS

There is an old saying: "A picture is worth a thousand words." This saying applies not only to life in general, but also to you as a cryptic ethical hacker. Show someone his or her password that you just captured because it wasn't encrypted and that person won't repeat the mistake. There are different packet capture tools you can use for this type of operation. Following is a list:

- AirMagnet: **www.airmagnet.com/**

- AiroPeek: **www.wildpackets.com/products/airopeek**

- AirScanner Mobile Sniffer: **http://airscanner.com/downloads/sniffer/sniffer.html**

- AirTraf: **http://airtraf.sourceforge.net/**

- CommView for WiFi: **https://goo.gl/toszRq**

- Capsa: **www.colasoft.com/products/capsa/index.php?id=754 30g**

- CENiffer: **www.epiphan.com/products_ceniffer.html**

- ethereal: **www.ethereal.com**

- Gulpit: **www.crak.com/gulpit.htm**

- KisMAC: **www.binaervarianz.de/projekte/programmieren/kis mac/**

- Kismet: **www.kismetwireless.net/**

- LANfielder: **www.wirelessvalley.com/**

- LinkFerret: **www.baseband.com/**

- Packetyzer: **https://goo.gl/KLiV1h**

- Mognet: **www.l0t3k.net/tools/Wireless/Mognet-1.16.tar.gz**

- ngrep: **www.remoteassessment.com/?op=pub_archive_searc h&query=wireless**

- Observer: **www.networkinstruments.com/**

- Sniffer Netasyst: **www.sniffer-netasyst.com/**

- Sniffer Wireless:
  www.networkgeneral.com/Products_details.aspx?Prd Id=20046178370181WEP

WEP/WPA CRACKING

Assuring yourself that you are totally protected because you use WPA or WEP is like saying, "Windows Defender is better than Norton Internet Security." Your WEP or WPA can be cracked because nothing is totally secure. Following are the tools you can use to crack WEP or WPA:

- Aircrack: **www.cr0.net:8040/code/network/**
- AirSnort: **http://sourceforge.net/projects/airsnort/**
- Destumbler:
  http://sourceforge.net/projects/destumbler
- Dwepcrack: **www.e.kth.se/~pvz/wifi/**
- jc-wepcracker:
  www.astalavista.com/?section=dir&cmd=file&id=3316
- Lucent Orinoco Registry Encryption/Decryption program:
  www.cqure.net/tools.jsp?id=3
- WepAttack: **http://wepattack.sourceforge.net/**
- WEPcrack: **http://sourceforge.net/projects/wepcrack/**
- WEPWedgie:
  http://sourceforge.net/projects/wepwedgie/
- WPA Cracker: **http://www.tinypeap.com/page8.html**
- WepLab: **http://weplab.sourceforge.net/**
- WinAirSnort: **www.nwp.nevillon.org/attack.html**

CRACKING PASSWORDS

Some tools out there can grab packets, look for passwords and amazingly, provide those passwords for you. These tools include:

> Dsniff (Windows port): **www.datanerds.net/~mike/dsniff.html**

> Dsniff (MacOS X port): **http://blafasel.org/~floh/ports/dsniff-2.3.osx.tgz**

> Cain & Abel: **www.oxid.it/cain.html**

> Dsniff: **www.monkey.org/~dugsong/dsniff/**

Don't forget the 10 Commandments of ethical hacking; make sure you crack the password you are authorized to crack. If you try to crack a password that is not meant to be cracked, you can end up in jail.

Dictionary Files and Word Lists

You can actually crack a password using a dictionary or word list. Most password crackers take a dictionary or a list of words and then encrypt the words. After the encryption, they compare the result to the password file. Then, the password is cracked successfully. Thus, you must seek out different wordlists or dictionaries. We have created a list of exceptional sources for wordlists and dictionaries:

> CERIAS Dictionaries and Wordlists: **ftp://ftp.cerias.purdue.edu/pub/dict**

> Default vendor passwords: **www.cirt.net/cgi-bin/passwd.pl**

> Outpost9 Wordlists: **www.outpost9.com/files/WordLists.html**

- PacketStorm   Wordlists: **http://packetstormsecurity.nl/Crackers/wordlists**

- University of Oxford Dictionaries and Wordlists: **ftp://ftp.ox.ac.uk/pub/wordlists**

GATHERING IP ADDRESSES AND SSIDs

Online blogs and other article directories say that you will be safer if you turn off your SSID broadcasting as a control, but this is essentially a fallacy. Many programs out there can help you get the SSIS of a system when it is turned off. They are:

- air-jack: **http://sourceforge.nct/projects/airjack/**

- Arping: **www.habets.pp.se/synscan/programs.php?prog=arping**

- essid_jack: **http://sourceforge.net/projects/airjack/**

- pong: **http://mobileaccess.de/wlan/index.html?go=technik&sid**

- SSIDsniff: **www.bastard.net/~kos/wifi/ssidsniff-0.40.tar.gz**

LEAP CRACKERS

You can find the acronyms of all of these terms in Appendix B of this book. EAP has been tagged as the solution to WEP authentication problems. On the other hand, what is tagged as being a protection has its own flaws as well. Following are the tools you can employ to help crack LEAP:

- anwrap: **http://packetstormsecurity.nl/cisco/anwrap.pl**

- asleap: **http://asleap.sourceforge.net/**

- THC-LEAPcracker: **http://thc.org/releases.php?s=4&q=&o**

NETWORK MAPPING

In the previous chapter, we discussed network mapping. After you have connected to an access point, you will want to have the network mapped. This is because you will want to know how many servers you can find and also what OS the server is running. You can use the following tools to map your network:

- Cheops: **www.marko.net/cheops/**

- Cheops-ng: **http://cheops-ng.sourceforge.net**

- SNMPUTIL.EXE: **www.microsoft.com**

- Snmpwalk: **www.trinux.org**

- Solarwinds Standard Edition Version: **www.solarwinds.net**

- WhatsUp Gold: **www.ipswitch.com/products/networkmanagement.html**

NETWORK SCANNERS

As the owner of a network, you should know everything that is going on with it. With the help of a network scanner, you will be able to identify the applications running on your network systems. You will likely find these applications on network devices and servers alike. Some of the tools we have used are:

- fping: www.fping.com

- GFI LANguard Network Security Scanner: **www.gfi.com/lannetscan**

- nessus: **www.nessus.org**

- nmap: **www.insecure.org/nmap**

- ➢ QualysGuard: **www.qualys.com**

- ➢ SoftPerfect Network Scanner: **www.softperfect.com/products/networkscanner**

- ➢ SuperScan: **www.foundstone.com/resources/proddesc/superscan. htm**

APPENDIX B: GLOSSARY OF ACRONYMS

- 3DES: Triple Data Encryption Standard
- ACK: Acknowledge ACL: Access Control List
- AES: Advanced Encryption Standard
- AES-CCMP: ES-Counter Mode CBC-MAC Protocol
- AES-WRAP: ES-Wireless Robust Authenticated Protocol
- AH: Authentication Header
- AP: Access Point
- BBWA: Broadband Wireless Access
- BER: Bit Error Rate BSS: Basic Service Set
- BSSID: Basic Service Set Identifier
- CCK: Complimentary Code Keying
- CF: Compact Flash
- CHAP: Challenge/Handshake Authentication Protocol
- CRC: Cyclic Redundancy Check
- CSMA/CA: Carrier Sense Multiple Access/Collision Avoidance
- CTS: Clear to Send
- DB: Decibel
- DBm: Decibel per milliwatt
- DBPSK: Differential Binary Phase Shifting Key
- DCF: Distributed Coordination Function
- DDoS: Distributed Denial of Service
- DES: Data Encryption Standard
- DHCP: Dynamic Host Configuration Protocol
- DiGLE: Delphi imaging Geographic Lookup Engine
- DMZ: De-Militarized Zone
- DoS: Denial of Service
- DQPSK: Differential Quadrature Phase Shifting Key
- DSSS: Direct Sequence Spread Spectrum

- EAP: Extensible Authentication Protocol
- EAPOL: EAP Over LANs
- EAP-TLS: AP-Transport Layer Security
- EAP-TTLS: EAP-Tunneled Transport Layer Security
- ESP: Encapsulating Security Protocol
- ESS: Extended Service Set
- ESSID: Extended Service Set Identifier
- FCC: Federal Communications Commission
- FH: Frequency Hopping
- FHSS: Frequency Hopping Spread Spectrum
- FIN: Finish
- GFSK: Gaussian Phase Shifting Key
- GHz: Gigahertz
- GPS: Global Positioning System
- GSM: Global System for Mobile Communications
- HR/DSSS: High-Rate Direct-Sequence Spread Spectrum
- HTTP: Hypertext Transfer Protocol
- IAPP: Inter-Access Point Protocol
- IBSS: Independent Basic Service Set
- ICAT: Internet Categorization of Attack Toolkit
- ICV: Integrity Check Value
- IDS: Intrusion Detection System
- IEEE: The Institute of Electrical and Electronics Engineers
- IETF: Internet Engineering Task Force
- IKE: Internet Key Exchange
- IP: Internet Protocol
- IPS: Intrusion Prevention System
- Ipsec: Internet Protocol Security
- ISM: Industrial, Scientific and Medical
- ISO: International Organization for Standardization
- IV: Initialization Vector

- JiGLE: Java-imaging Geographic Lookup Engine
- Kbps: Kilobits per second
- KHz: Kilohertz
- L2TP: Layer 2 Tunneling Protocol
- LAN: Local Area Network
- LBT: Listen Before Talking
- LDAP: Lightweight Directory Access Protocol
- LEAP: Lightweight EAP
- LLC: Logical Link Control
- LOS: Line of Sight
- MAC: Media Access Control
- Mbps: Megabits per second
- MD5: Message Digest 5
- MHz: Megahertz
- MIB: Management Information Base
- MIC: Message Integrity Check
- MIMO: Multiple-In/Multiple-Out
- MITM: Man-in-the-Middle; Monkey-in-the-Middle
- mW: Milliwatt
- NIC: Network Interface Card
- OFDM: Orthogonal Frequency Division Multiplexing
- PAP: Password Authentication Protocol
- PCF: Point Coordination Function
- PCMCIA: Personal Computer Memory Card International Association
- PDA: Personal Digital Assistant
- PEAP: Protected EAP
- PED: Personal Electronic Device
- PKI: Public-Key Infrastructure
- PoE: Power over Ethernet
- PPTP: Point-to-Point Tunneling Protocol
- PSK: Pre-Shared Key

- PS-Poll: Power Save Poll
- QAM: Quadrature Amplitude Modulation
- RADIUS: Remote Authentication Dial-in User Service
- RBAC: Role-Based Access Control
- RC4: Ron's Code 4
- RF LOS: Radio Frequency Line of Sight
- RF: Radio Frequency
- RSA: Rivest-Shamir-Adelman
- RSN: Robust Security Networks
- RTS: Request to Send
- SME: Small-to-Medium Enterprise
- SNMP: Simple Network Management Protocol
- SNR: Signal-to-Noise Ratio
- SOHO: Small Office Home Office
- SSH: Secure Shell
- SSID: Service Set Identifier
- SSL: Secure Sockets Layer
- SYN: Synchronize
- TCP/IP: Transmission Control Protocol/Internet Protocol
- TCP: Transmission Control Protocol
- THC: The Hacker's Choice
- TKIP: Temporal Key Integrity Protocol
- TLS: Transport Layer Security
- UDP: User Datagram Protocol
- USB: Universal Serial Bus
- VPN: Virtual Private Network
- WAP: Wireless Application Protocol
- WEP: Wired Equivalent Privacy
- Wi-Fi: Wireless Fidelity
- WLAN: Wireless Local Area Network
- WIDS: Wireless Intrusion Detection System

- WiGLE: Wireless Geographic Logging Engine
- WISP: Wireless Internet Service Provider
- WMM: Wi-Fi Multimedia
- WPA: Wi-Fi Protected Access

PREVIEW OF THE BEST SELLING BOOK "CRYPTOCURRENCY" BY ABRAHAM K WHITE

INTRODUCTION

First, scribbles on stones overshadowed pictorial writing on caves. As soon as humankind learned how to produce paper and better ink, scrolls quickly overcame stones. Then came the age of typewriters. Not even a century later, digital images and computer-based writing have become the fastest and easiest medium to share and store information.

Although it is remarkably revolutionary, the advent of digital currency represents just a fraction of the innovations the computer age has ushered in. While some schools of thought have said that digital currencies will not be sustainable in the long term, others have simply jumped on board the train to reap its existing advantages.

Many innovations have been successfully integrated into the modern world, so one cannot state that cryptocurrencies are completely unreliable. The world continues to evolve.

Time remains the only factor that can determine the boom or doom of any innovation.

CHAPTER 1: THE BASICS OF CRYPTOGRAPHIC CURRENCY

In basic terms, cryptocurrencies are virtual monies within a computer system. They are a series of digital records held by multiple parties, which track the amount of currency that individual wallets hold. A cryptocurrency can be said to be an asset which has been digitally designed to function as a medium of exchange. A cryptocurrency uses cryptography to protect and enhance transactions and to manage the inclusion of more units of that particular currency. Widely considered as alternatives to real currencies, cryptocurrencies are commonly referred to as digital currencies.

Matthew Field and Cara McGoogan, correspondents from the British newspaper The Telegraph, said that cryptocurrencies are types of private, virtual money intended to be adequately protected at all times. Cryptocurrencies are linked to the net and created using cryptographic processes. Their creation also involves the conversion of information into codes that are very difficult to crack, which essentially monitor their exchanges throughout the network.

Field and McGoogan said that originally, cryptographic procedures developed out of the need to protect the transmission of news and information during World War II. In the modern digital world, it metamorphosed into the foundation for the online distribution of private and protected information, with the help of advanced knowledge in computer science and more complex mathematical calculations.

Cryptocurrencies are usually referred to as "digital gold" because through preservation, they increase in value over time. As a medium of payment, cryptocurrencies are easy and convenient to use around the globe. Because transactions using cryptocurrencies are generally transparent, they also operate as a medium of payment in illegal transactions or activities.

Cryptocurrencies have given a massive kickstart to a new and rapidly growing marketplace. For instance, Poloniex (an exchange platform) has assisted in the trading of countless cryptocurrencies since they surfaced. Many of these exchange platforms experience larger percentages of trades than some European stock exchanges.

HAVE CRYPTOCURRENCIES LIVED UP TO THE HYPE?

One can say that a large percentage of the world's population is still very skeptical about the practicability of cryptocurrencies as a medium of economic exchange. However, the number of investors is increasing daily.

Many monetary policies put in place by governments have suffered setbacks due to cryptocurrencies because the latter are forms of money whose supplies are controlled and monitored without any interference from banks or financial institutions. Policies to manipulate inflation and deflation simply cannot work with cryptocurrencies.

A public speaker, Sarah Granger, once said that although cryptocurrencies are still not stable and are relatively new compared to gold, they are gaining ground and will likely undergo developmental tweaks in the near future. Granger said that cryptocurrencies became more popular in terms of awareness and acceptability as uncertainty plagued the post-election period. Granger also said that cryptocurrencies should be made easily available for adoption on a large scale, which would include the strengthening of security and safety provisions for investors and other users. In conclusion, Granger said that in a few years, the world will have advanced to a stage in which everyone is able to keep or hide their money with the help of cryptocurrencies, knowing that anywhere they go, their money will be within reach.

The invention of the first cryptocurrency, Bitcoin, marked a revolution in digital money, as early attempts to develop such technologies hadn't drawn much attention. Even Satoshi Nakamoto, the inventor of the blockchain on which Bitcoin thrives, did not envision the cryptocurrency's popularity. Bitcoin instantly caused a stir, and by the end of the first quarter of 2015 hundreds of cryptocurrencies were in existence.

A group of individuals–generally referred to as "miners"– balance ledgers, make modifications and are responsible for the general safekeeping of cryptocurrency platforms. Miners are experts who, using computers, timestamp as well as validate transactions by adding ledgers in a specific pattern to the system. These ledgers are assumed to be secure because of the belief that miners are financially motivated to keep the ledgers running.

Cryptocurrencies are essentially developed to reduce the manufacturing of national currencies. This, in turn, will limit the total value of currency in circulation. In 2008, Satoshi Nakamoto, the inventor of Bitcoin, was quoted as saying that his intentions were not to invent a currency. Instead, he had planned to develop a peer-to-peer electronic cash system.

Satoshi's invention was a breakthrough in the creation of digital money because he devised a way to build a decentralized digital system. Before him, there had been failed attempts to develop digital money. After observing the principal causes of these failures, Satoshi eliminated the idea of a centrally controlled system. Instead, he built a peer-to-peer network system. Decentralization caused the rise of cryptocurrency.

Digital cash was attained through a payment network with transactions and balances. However, a key issue that required resolution was the continuous stoppage of double spending. This was accomplished through a central server that contained all the balance details.

However, because a decentralized network has no central server, every entity on the network is responsible for storing and balancing records. Each peer has a record and a list containing all the transactions to ascertain the validity of future transactions.

In a decentralized network, the server is not present. Therefore, each entity in the network must do its part. Every peer in the network requires information about all of the transactions to determine whether all the forthcoming transactions are legitimate.

When peers encounter a dispute regarding a small balance, the transaction breaks down. A need exists for absolute agreement but the question remains: "How can a network without a central authority have a uniform agreement?"

No one could answer this question, and it appeared impossible to achieve. Satoshi eventually solved the problem. His solution was to obtain absolute agreement without the inclusion of a central authority. Eventually, the actualization of his aspirations played a major role in the success of digital currencies.

In 2009, Satoshi, who at the time was anonymous, created the premier decentralized cryptocurrency known as Bitcoin. It used a cryptographic hash function (SHA-256) as proof of its work scheme, which was based on the Tangle. Since then, many other cryptocurrencies have been introduced, but many have not been as successful as Bitcoin, as they offer little or no improvement in comparison. Curiosity about the Bitcoin phenomenon forced the treasury department in the UK to conduct a study on cryptocurrencies in 2014. The government wanted to know how cryptocurrencies could help develop the economy and whether appropriate regulations should be adopted with respect to their use.

STRONGHOLDS

An excerpt from Coin Pursuit states that virtual currencies such as Bitcoin are not governed by the rules and regulations of banks, financial institutions or governments. Digital currencies do not involve transaction fees or various other bank-related charges.

With respect to virtual coins, a "cold war" has been waged against fees, some of which are so effectively embedded that they cannot be confirmed. Additionally, in cases of inflation, national or government-supported currencies tend to lose their value. However, such situations do not necessarily diminish the value of digital currencies.

Due to their characteristics, cryptocurrencies have withstood criticisms. Some of these characteristics are:

UNIVERSALITY: The physical location of users or investors has no influence on transactions, as activities are linked globally through a network of computers on the internet. There is no need to physically meet any participant once a smooth flow of operations is established.

INSTANT TRANSACTIONS: In cryptocurrency deals, the initiation and confirmation of transactions is carried out almost instantly. Once every detail has been placed in the network, business is completed within seconds.

GUARANTEED SAFETY: Cryptocurrencies are securely stored using a cryptography system. This means that investors have unique private keys which serve as authentication for any transaction. The provision of constant random cryptographic numbers makes it impossible to steal or divert cryptocurrencies from users' accounts.

UNRESTRICTED ACCESS: Cryptocurrencies are readily available for anyone's use. No permission whatsoever is needed before transactions occur. Cryptocurrencies are accessible without restrictions.

ANONYMITY: Cryptocurrency accounts and transactions are not linked to real-life identities. The addresses shown during transactions are series of randomly generated characters which belong to other participants. While these addresses are used to monitor and analyze the flow of transactions, they do not necessarily correlate with the users' actual addresses.

THE EDGE OVER FIAT CURRENCIES

Some experts with the central bank have said that the consistent use of cryptocurrencies will reduce the bank's power to influence credit prices. According to these experts, the possibility also exists that a consumer's confidence in fiat currencies will drop significantly as cryptocurrencies gain more ground.

Banking officer Gareth Murphy said that agencies that compile statistical analyses of economies will experience great difficulty carrying out such tasks as cryptocurrencies become more popular. This would become a major challenge for governments, as such data is used to control their economies. Furthermore, Murphy warned that cryptocurrencies will reduce the central bank's grip on exchange rates and other money-related policies.

By 2016, almost all of the large accounting firms and popular computer science companies had researched cryptocurrencies and what could be gained from them. Publications and projects have sought to understand the full potential of cryptocurrencies.

At present, many have come to understand cryptocurrencies as milestone advancements in the finance sector. Already, governments, banks and financial institutions are aware of their importance.

Basel Ismail, a cryptocurrency geek, FinTech leader, Cornell MBA and Norwich InfoSec, said that the increased use of cryptocurrencies for commercial purposes, along with the introduction of other educational and developmental activities, can improve people's knowledge of the functions of a blockchain, the meaning of Bitcoin and the ways in which virtual tokens and currencies can assist individuals, thereby boosting the technology's popularity and polishing its image.

WHAT MINERS DO

Bob Mason (FX Empire) said that the cryptocurrency mining procedure is not the same as the mining procedure for valuables like silver and gold because the mining of cryptocurrencies doesn't yield physical assets. He said that while the mining of cryptocurrencies involves an electronic process and requires electronic wallets, commodity mining like that for gold usually involves searching for, digging up and excavating physical objects. However, the cryptocurrency mining process could, to an extent, be likened to investing in the future markets of valuables rather than currently visible ones.

Even if it is done through a cloud mining process from a service provider, through the purchasing of private mining software or through a data platform, the mining of cryptocurrency creates new sets of a digital currency in relation to the exact platform on which the procedure is being carried out. The mining process involves a lot of computation and becomes complex as its corresponding platform progresses. Some mining processes are already involved in finding solutions for cryptographic puzzles and consume lots of computer-related power.

Essentially, miners are experts within a cryptocurrency network and are responsible for the creation of currencies and the confirmation of transactions. To understand these tasks, a need exists to digest their databases' technicalities. Bitcoin, for instance, is a system of collaborators and records of all transactions kept by each collaborator. This ensures a balance of each account on the network or system. Simply put, when a file states that User A has given a certain amount of Bitcoin to User B, it gets signed by User A's private key. After the file has been authenticated, a transaction is directed from one peer to the other through a broadcast in the network. That is the basis of the peer-to-peer technology.

The entire network is instantly aware of this transaction. This is the stage at which miners play a crucial role, as the confirmation of such transactions would trigger the awareness.

It is important to note that confirmation is a crucial stage in cryptocurrency deals. In fact, cryptocurrencies thrive only on that basis. An unconfirmed transaction can be altered because it would still be on a pending list. However, once it gets confirmed, it cannot be reversed or tampered with. It instantly becomes a permanent record of the blockchain's transactions.

Miners are the only people who validate transactions. That's their primary responsibility in a cryptocurrency platform. They verify transactions by stamping and subsequently broadcasting them within the network. Once a miner confirms a transaction, all nodes must add it to their databases. It eventually becomes part of the blockchain. The miner receives tokens as a form of payment for their important role in the network. Interestingly, anyone can become a miner. The decentralized nature of the blockchain network makes it impossible to assign the mining tasks to specific sets of users. So that it can work for a long period, a cryptocurrency network cannot afford to restrict mining activities to a particular group, as this would increase the probability of abuse. The system would face destruction should a miner broadcast fake transactions across peers throughout the network. This is why Satoshi created a policy in which miners must find a way to connect new blocks with their predecessors through a cryptographic product referred to as a hash. This process is called Proof-of-Work. It has a hash algorithm of SHA 256. While it is not necessarily important to know all the technicalities of SHA 256, it is necessary to understand that it is more like a cryptologic puzzle from which miners constantly seek answers. Once the puzzle has been solved, a miner builds a block and adds it to the blockchain. The miner is then permitted to add a coinbase transaction, which ultimately earns the miner crypto cash.

To an extent, miners believe that mining is an interesting process which gives them the opportunity to acquire knowledge of complex electronic procedures.

Brian Roemmele, an alchemist and metaphysician, said that many of his friends in the technology sector already had knowledge of coding or ideas about the procedures and steps they were to follow. He said that currently it isn't easy to find individuals who understand what is happening with the hardware component for which they are writing codes. Roemmele mentioned that the mining process for algorithm-based currencies allows miners to realize the core importance of hardware components, which is enticing.

Made in the USA
Coppell, TX
13 June 2023

18063212R00128